HISTORY AND THE ECONOMIC PAST

HISTORY
AND THE
ECONOMIC PAST

*An Account of the Rise and Decline
of Economic History in Britain*

D. C. COLEMAN

CLARENDON PRESS · OXFORD
1987

Oxford University Press, Walton Street, Oxford OX2 6DP

Oxford New York Toronto
Delhi Bombay Calcutta Madras Karachi
Petaling Jaya Singapore Hong Kong Tokyo
Nairobi Dar es Salaam Cape Town
Melbourne Auckland
and associated companies in
Beirut Berlin Ibadan Nicosia

Oxford is a trade mark of Oxford University Press

Published in the United States
by Oxford University Press, New York

British Library Cataloguing in Publication Data
Coleman, D. C.
History and the economic past: an account
of the rise and decline of economic history
in Britain.
1. Economic history—Great Britain—
History
330′.9   HC28.5.G7
ISBN 0-19-828305-9

Library of Congress Cataloging in Publication Data
Coleman, D. C. (Donald Cuthbert), 1920–
History and the economic past.
Includes index.
1. Economic history—Study and teaching—Great Britain.
I. Title.
HC28.5.G7C65 1987   330′.07′1041   86-28543
ISBN 0-19-828305-9

Printed in Great Britain by
Billing & Sons, Limited, Worcester

Contents

I

Introduction

'What I was going to say was—I wonder if you will consider taking some other subject as well as the classics? History, for example, preferably economic history?'

'No, headmaster.'

Evelyn Waugh, *Scott-King's Modern Europe* (1946)

JUST at the time when Waugh's fictional classics master was declining to take on the teaching of economic history, that subject was about to experience a remarkable surge of popularity in Britain. Uniquely amongst the varieties of history, its arrival in favour was to be signalled in the course of two or three decades by the creation of numerous separate university departments devoted to it; by a flowering of professors professing it; and by many boys and girls sitting papers in English economic history at Ordinary or Advanced level in their General Certificate of Education examinations. The social extent of this phenomenon must not of course be exaggerated. That majority of the British population who did not attend university or stay on long enough at school would have had little clear or specific idea what economic history was. At an academic and scholarly level, however, the boom was real.

Equally real was its subsequent collapse as the blessings of popularity demonstrated the perils they embody. By the 1970s a variety of indicators were signalling not only that the upswing was at an end but that decline was setting in. Symptoms of complacency could be detected in some quarters; critical comment heralding doom came from others. One distinguished expatriate, writing in 1976, foresaw the likelihood that the

1

'isolation of British economic historians both from non-economic historians and from professional economists may in the long run lead to introversion and sterility'.[1] Self-searching began. Investigation of numbers taking the subject at A level suggested in 1985 that if current trends continued 'economic history might disappear before the end of the century'.[2] Seen by some history students as a soft option, it had attracted the mediocre; seen by others as too difficult because of its increasingly 'economic' character, it had suffered a drop in entries. In any event orthodox political history remained 'the choice of the élite'. So economic history appeared as clearly getting 'the worst of both worlds'.[3] Then for those reading history at university sundry burgeoning new varieties of 'social' history were proving seductive; and for bright young economists, happy with numbers and theory, economic history seemed to offer neither intellectual rewards nor the promise of lucrative jobs.

Upswing and downturn: how had they come about? How, indeed, had the subject come into being as an area deemed worthy of scholarly enquiry? What had been its relationships with its two ill-matched parents, history and economics?

Having spent the forty years since 1946 variously engaged in studying, teaching, and contributing to the subject, I had come to wonder whether it really existed or, to be more accurate, whether it should exist in the form which it had assumed in Britain. So it seemed a suitable retirement pursuit to try to put together some answers to these questions. The account which follows is concerned almost entirely with the British experience; it may thus shed some light on this particular variant of the British disease. It deals not at all with

[1] L. Stone, 'History and the Social Sciences' in his *The Past and the Present* (1981), p. 14. The article was originally published in C. Delzell (ed.), *The Future of History* (Nashville, Tenn., 1976). (The place of publication of all books referred to is London unless otherwise stated).

[2] R. G. Wilson and J. F. Hadwin, 'Economic and Social History at Advanced Level', *Economic History Review* 2nd Ser. xxxviii (1985), p. 566.

[3] Ibid., p. 554.

the philosophy of history and is only marginally involved with such large issues as the methodology of the social sciences. It lays no claim to be as wide-ranging or so searching as Geoffrey Hawthorn's history of sociology although the title at least of his book, *Enlightenment and Despair*, may evoke some echoing responses.[4] Today, any sort of study which has its roots in the optimistic rationalism of the Enlightenment cannot but experience at least a modicum of disillusion. Economic history is no exception. But hope remains; and a better appreciation of the subject's divergent and quarrelsome parents may help in the process of reconciliation.

Disillusionment has not been relieved by the advent in Britain, over the past decade, of government measures aimed at reducing public expenditure on education. The study of history in some schools is being curtailed; the reduction in university and polytechnic funding is targeted especially at the humanities and social sciences; the budget of the Economic and Social Research Council, after the failure of an attempt to abolish it completely, has been cut. All this has become well known. It is not, however, a particular consideration of this book, because the trends examined in Chapter 6 were becoming evident before these measures were announced and well before they began to take effect. The measures certainly add to the practical problems facing economic historians, but their possible consequences have not been taken into account in the discussion in Chapter 7 of some future desiderata.

A small amount of the material in Chapters 5–7 was used in my inaugural lecture at Cambridge University in 1972[5] and in the course of an unpublished public lecture, 'The Rise and Decline of Economic History', given at the London School of Economics in 1981. I am grateful to these two institutions for offering the occasion for the two lectures. Having spent

---

[4] Geoffrey Hawthorn, *Enlightenment and Despair: A History of Sociology* (Cambridge, 1976).
[5] *What has happened to Economic History?* (Cambridge, 1972).

virtually the whole of my academic life within their walls I owe them both an immeasurable debt. Such critical comments as are to be found in this book are not made in any spirit of antagonism but rather in the friendly hope of stimulating some reform and renewal in what seem to me to be desirable directions.

2

Scottish Enlightenment

Can we expect that a government will be well modelled by a people who know not how to make a spinning-wheel, or to employ a loom to advantage?

David Hume, 'Of Refinement in the Arts' in *Political Discourses* (1752)

THE origins of economic history as a subject of study in Britain are to be found in eighteenth-century Scotland. The writings of the Scottish Enlightenment, and more specifically of the Scottish historical school, provided the first British signpost to the examination of the economic past as an essential element in the understanding of human society.

The works of David Hume, Sir James Steuart, and Adam Smith, along with those of William Robertson, Adam Ferguson, and John Millar have been, jointly or severally, the subject of much learned study and exegesis. Analysis of them has examined their contributions to economics and sociology, to political thought and philosophy, as well as to historiography in general; they have been put into the context of such contemporaries as Gibbon or Bolingbroke and of their continental European antecedents and parallels—Montesquieu, Voltaire, Cantillon, Turgot, the Physiocrats, and Vico. It is not my purpose to pursue these lines of enquiry. My more limited aim is to look briefly at their role as progenitors of what was much later to be called 'economic history', a term unknown to the eighteenth century.

It may well be true, as has been said, that to all such writers 'the improvement of wealth, the discovery of useful arts, the elaboration of industrial technique, and the creation and preservation of appropriate social institutions' were of much more interest than dynasties, wars, great men, and other items of the stock-in-trade of conventional historians.[1] Yet the significance which they accorded in practice to economic phenomena varied greatly. William Robertson, one of the more orthodox members of the Scottish school, writing in 1769, put some emphasis on the 'progress of commerce' in 'polishing the manners of the European nations and in leading them to order, equal laws and humanity'. After the barbarians, there had come the Italians, the Hanse, and then the English to help spur the revival of trade; and thereby to help 'wear off those prejudices which maintain distinctions and animosity between nations'.[2] Despite their historical context, however, such generalities did not go much further than the sundry encomiums on the glories of commerce which had become commonplace utterances from the later seventeenth century onwards.

In the 1670s, for example, John Evelyn had been extolling 'the miracles of commerce' which had 'taught us Religion, instructed us in Polity, cultivated our Manners, and furnished us with the Delicacies of virtuous and happy Living'.[3] Merchants themselves were praised as spreaders of international peace and light. They stimulated employment and knit mankind together 'in a mutual intercourse of good office'; and, 'by mutual benefits', they diffused 'mutual love from pole to pole'.[4] Such sentiments were not much reinforced by appeals to the past. Nor did some of the more interesting arguments used by contemporary writers in seeking reasons for economic growth necessarily demand, or get, an historical

---

[1] H. R. Trevor-Roper, 'The Historical Philosophy of the Enlightenment', *Studies on Voltaire and the Eighteenth Century* vol. xxvii (Geneva, 1963), pp. 1667–87.

[2] William Robertson, *The Progress of Society in Europe* (1779; ed. F. Gilbert, Chicago, 1972) pp. 63, 67. This was the introductory volume of Robertson's *History of the Reign of Charles V.*

[3] John Evelyn, *Navigation and Commerce* (1674), p. 11.

[4] Anon., *The Character and Qualifications of an Honest Loyal Merchant* (1686), p. 2; Joseph Addison, *The Spectator* No. 69 (19 May 1711), quoted H. R. Fox Bourne, *English Merchants* (1886), pp. 205–6; George Lillo, *The London Merchant* (1731; ed. Bonamy Dobrée, 1948), p. 41.

dimension. Neither Dudley North in 1691 ('The main spur to Trade, or rather to Industry and Ingenuity is the exorbitant Appetites of Men . . . did Men content themselves with bare Necessaries, we should have a poor World') nor, later, Bernard Mandeville, in the *Fable of the Bees*, sought to provide historical backing for their particular appeals to consumer demand as a force in economic advance.[5] The merits of competition in commerce ('necessity and emulation'), likewise found in North and Mandeville but particularly praised by Henry Martin in a celebrated tract anticipating, in 1701, the economic advocacy of a later age, gave themselves even less to historical illustration.[6] Sir William Temple's chapter on trade in his *Observations upon the United Provinces* makes the dimension of economic history rather more evident. His materialistic argument that 'the true original and ground of Trade' was the 'great multitude of people crowding into small compass of land' is given rather more support than the obligatory classical references and a nod at Venice. Links between political order and commercial progress in the history of the United Provinces are made explicit, albeit sketchily; and Dutch success in trade is found to be 'no effect of common contrivances, of natural dispositions or scituations, or of trivial accidents; But of a great concurrence of Circumstances, a long course of Time, force of Orders and Method . . .'.[7]

Such an invitation to the writing of economic history was not accepted in Britain until David Hume began to put economic and social change into his account of the past. In Hume the existing commonplace that commerce was generally beneficent in promoting international understanding

[5] Dudley North, *Discourses upon Trade* (1691) reprinted in J. R. McCulloch (ed.), *Early English Tracts on Commerce* (1856; repr. Cambridge, 1952), p. 528. Bernard Mandeville, *The Fable of the Bees* (1714–24; ed. P. Harth, Harmondsworth, 1970).

[6] [Henry Martin], *Considerations on the East India Trade* (1701) in McCulloch (ed.), *Early Tracts*, especially pp. 561–2, 568. On Martin's authorship see Christine Macleod, 'Henry Martin and the Authorship of *Considerations on the East India Trade*', *Bulletin of the Institute of Historical Research* LVI (1983), pp. 222–9.

[7] Sir William Temple, *Observations upon the United Provinces of the Netherlands* (1673; ed. G. N. Clark, Cambridge, 1971), pp. 109, 118.

was extended to present the growth of commerce and industry as a crucial element in the advance of civilization; it was responsible for improvements in government, order, and liberty. He sketched the model in his *Political Discourses* of 1752:

Laws, order, police, discipline—these can never be carried to any degree of perfection before human reason has refined itself by exercise, and by an application to the more vulgar arts, at least, of commerce and manufactures. Can we expect that a government will be well modelled by a people who know not how to make a spinning-wheel, or to employ a loom to advantage?[8]

History revealed that foreign trade had generally preceded 'refinement in home manufactures and given birth to domestic luxury'.[9] This in turn helped to generate 'that middling rank of men who are the best and firmest basis of public liberty'.[10] And so to the House of Commons, 'the support of our popular government and all the world acknowledges that it owed its chief influence and consideration to the increase of commerce, which threw such a balance of property into the hands of the commons'.[11] With the study of the vulgar arts of commerce and manufactures thus advocated, economic history may seem to be in sight, and the economic interpretation of the Civil War—so fashionable in the mid-twentieth century—perceivable on the horizon.

However, despite his concern with the historical significance of such economic phenomena, Hume did not accord them a central place in the narrative when he came to write his *History*. Certainly he wrote what the eighteenth century called 'philosophical history'.[12] But matters economic and

[8] David Hume, 'Of Refinement in the Arts', in *Political Discourses* (1752; ed. W. B. Robertson, 1908), p. 19.
[9] 'Of Commerce', ibid., p. 11.
[10] 'Of Refinement', ibid., p. 23.
[11] Ibid.
[12] Hume, *The History of Great Britain: The Reigns of James I and Charles I* (1754; ed. Duncan Forbes, Harmondsworth, 1970), Introduction, p. 14.

social were given special, separate, and limited treatment. He did not provide a Harringtonian interpretation of English history since the sixteenth century. The rise of the landed gentry and of the power of the Commons were obvious enough and got little further comment. In his first and most important volume, for example, they are effectively confined to the Appendix to the reign of James I. He saw this procedure as needing a special word of explanation:

It may not be improper, at this period to make a pause; and, departing a little from the historical style, take a survey of the state of the kingdom, with regard to government, manners, finances, arms, trade, learning. Where a just notion is not formed of these particulars, history can be very little instructive, and often will not be intelligible.[13]

A century later, Macaulay's celebrated third chapter, for all its differences, had something of the same separateness: both were interludes in an historical narrative.

Before making the obvious move on to Adam Smith, it is time to look briefly at Sir James Steuart who, in so many ways, stood apart from what might be called the 'Glasgow group' of the Scottish Enlightenment. His position in society, his experience of life, his approach to political economy: all were different. And, more immediately relevant to the present purpose, so was his attitude to the past. He was never an historian in the sense that both Hume and Millar were. Nor did he use the economic past as a basis for the formulation of theory in the manner of Smith. In his *Political Œconomy* he provided historical examples, but history of the 'philosophical' sort, although sometimes making an appearance, did not play a major part in his argument. He did, however, draw upon recent French history and upon Petty and Davenant for data on English population; and he provided very specific historical accounts, complete with statistics, in the section of

---

[13] Hume, *History*, p. 219.

the work dealing with coinage, credit, and public finance in general.[14] Indeed, these chapters exhibit a use of historical material of a much more detailed and quantitative nature than anything in Smith, Hume, or Millar.

Smith, in contrast, expressed scepticism about the value of political arithmetic and has virtually no quantitative treatment at all of economic phenomena, past or present, which he analysed.[15] Yet, although he apparently scorned statistics and never attempted the writing of narrative history in the manner of Hume, Robertson, or Millar, his use of history was an integral feature of his analysis, evident in all his writings. He employed both the orthodox kind of history and the 'philosophical' or what Dugald Stewart called the 'theoretical or conjectural' sort.[16] The two were sometimes in conflict. As has been observed, the conflict is especially evident in Book III of the *Wealth of Nations* in the 'distinction between the speculative historical progress of opulence and the orthodox historical progress'.[17] Something called 'the natural progress of things' had to be equipped with an appropriate account of the historical progress of things. The dilemma thereby generated is still with the economic historian today.

Smith's 'philosophical' history was built up from a number of crucial themes or assumptions.[18] Four may be singled out. First, there was the psychological assumption of continuously operating self-interest, not simply in the sense of 'economic

[14] Sir James Steuart, *An Inquiry into the Principles of Political Œconomy* (1767; ed. A. S. Skinner, 2 vols., Edinburgh, 1966). See e.g. vol. I, pp. 51–9, 98–116; vol. II, pp. 532–63, 604–47. Also S. R. Sen, *The Economics of Sir James Steuart* (1957), p. 21.

[15] Adam Smith, *An Inquiry into the Nature and Causes of the Wealth of Nations* (1776; ed. E. Cannan, Modern Library edn., New York, 1937), p. 501. The nearest approach to a quantitative treatment is provided by some figures relating to bounties on the herring fishery in chap. 5 of Book IV and the Appendix thereto.

[16] Dugald Stewart, *Account of the Life and Writings of Adam Smith, LL.D.* (1794) in W. P. D. Wightman, J. C. Bryce, and I. S. Ross (eds.), *Adam Smith: Essays on Philosophical Subjects* (Oxford, 1980), p. 293.

[17] *Wealth of Nations* (eds. R. H. Campbell and A. S. Skinner, 2 vols., Oxford, 1976), I, pp. 55–6.

[18] On Smith as historian, see the invaluable essay by A. S. Skinner, 'Adam Smith: an Economic Interpretation of History' in A. S. Skinner and T. Wilson (eds.), *Essays on Adam Smith* (Oxford, 1975), pp. 154–78.

man' or of a rationalistic Benthamite calculus,[19] but in the widest sense of self-betterment. 'The desire of bettering our condition' was with us from the womb to the grave:[20]

The uniform, constant and uninterrupted effort of every man to better his condition, the principle from which public and national, as well as private opulence is originally derived is frequently powerful enough to maintain the natural progress of things towards improvement, in spite both of the extravagance of government and of the greatest errors of administration.[21]

The word 'frequently' in this passage will serve to introduce the second theme. Individual self-interest, by the working of the invisible hand, had the unforeseen and unintended consequence of leading to social benefit through the creation of wealth. But it did not always have its own way: it had to battle at times against the 'extravagance of government' or against the wiles, jealousy, and 'monopolizing spirit' of merchants and manufacturers, who invented the mercantile system and foisted it on governments. The conflict between Smith as orthodox historian and as 'philosophical' historian, indeed the weakness of the former in seeking to support the latter, is again evident in his treatment of the mercantile system in Book IV of the *Wealth of Nations*. The second theme may, however, be summarized thus: self-interest was historically conducive to the 'progress of opulence', via the operation of unforeseen consequences, but that progress was periodically checked by the actions of governments or businessmen.

The third theme helping to build up the complex symphony of his 'philosophical' history is the notion of economic growth in stages—hunting, pasturage, farming and commerce—that growth itself being strongly influenced, even determined, by

[19] See D. Winch, *Adam Smith's Politics* (Cambridge, 1978), pp. 167–9, 181.

[20] *Wealth of Nations* (ed. Cannan), p. 324. Belief in the existence of such a desire was not new to Smith. In the 1690s Gregory King had written of 'the Natural Propensity of the People to improve and better their Condition' in the manuscript known as the 'Burns Journal', printed in facsimile in P. Laslett (ed.), *The Earliest Classics: John Graunt and Gregory King* (Pioneers of demography series, 1973), p. 162.

[21] *Wealth of Nations* (ed. Cannan), p. 326.

physical environment. Just how fundamental this theme was to Smith's vision of economic change is a matter of some dispute. From one vantage point it appears as an 'organizing principle'; from another merely 'a loose framework'.[22] From one it is notable for 'the almost Marxian reliance which is placed on economic forces'; from another, 'modes of subsistence exert an influence on the pattern of events, if at all, only when coupled with other factors which include favourable geographical conditions, historical accidents, and even the personalities of monarchs'.[23] Suffice to note that the historical model-building represented by this stage theory is clearly present (e.g. in the *Lectures on Jurisprudence* and in Books III and V of the *Wealth of Nations*) but it is not explicitly and continuously employed as the sole basis upon which to build a view of the economic past. In that view, just as he invokes the Tartars as an example of a people fixed in an economic state by their environment ('As the Tartars have been always a nation of shepherds, which they will always be from the nature of their country . . .'),[24] so he offers the growth of towns as the crucial historical agent of transition from the third, agricultural, stage to his fourth stage, that of commerce, i.e. the exchange economy. And in that process he has room for the self-interested pursuit of both political and economic ends as productive of the unforeseen transition.

The last, and in some ways the most important, of the main items in his vision of historical progress is everything that can be summed up within the embracing theme of 'commerce and liberty'. Enunciated earlier by Hume, it was extended and deepened by Smith; a vital political dimension was added to the historical picture of self-bettering man.[25] The classic state-

[22] Cf. R. L. Meek, 'Smith, Turgot and the "Four Stages" Theory', *History of Political Economy* III (1971), pp. 9–27; and Winch, *Adam Smith's Politics*, p. 63.

[23] Cf. Skinner in Skinner and Wilson (eds.), *Essays*, p. 155 and Winch, ibid.

[24] Adam Smith, *Lectures on Jurisprudence* (eds. R. L. Meek, D. D. Raphael, and P. G. Stein, Oxford, 1978), p. 220.

[25] See Duncan Forbes, 'Sceptical Whiggism, Commerce and Liberty' in Skinner and Wilson (eds.), *Essays*, pp. 193–4.

ment of the theme is in Book III, after he has provided his historical sketch of the rise of towns contributing to the 'natural progress of opulence' in the countries to which they belonged.

Commerce and manufactures gradually introduced order and good government, and with them, the liberty and security of individuals, among the inhabitants of the country, who had before lived almost in a continual state of war with their neighbours and of servile dependency upon their superiors. This, though it has been least observed, is by far the most important of all their effects.[26]

The theme is thereafter developed at some length and incorporated into various parts of the *Wealth of Nations*. Right or wrong, it offered a linkage between what would today be called economic history and political history, a linkage which later generations of orthodox economists and historians in Britain were to succeed in severing almost completely.

Smith attributed the awareness of this most important of all the effects of the growth of commerce and manufactures to Hume, 'the only writer who, so far as I know, has hitherto taken notice of it'.[27] As has been pointed out, this is, on the face of it, an odd remark, because, by the time that the *Wealth of Nations* was published, the theme had already been taken up in print by others of the same school, for example, Adam Ferguson, Lord Kames, and, most notable for my present concern, John Millar.[28] A pupil and friend of Smith's, Millar had published his *Origins of the Distinction of Ranks* in 1771. The importance of this work in the early development of sociology has been acknowledged. Suffice here to emphasize that it, too, stressed the power to effect social and political transformation which was inherent in the growth of commerce and manufactures. It took the concept of stages of economic subsistence

---

[26] *Wealth of Nations* (ed. Cannan), p. 385.
[27] Ibid.
[28] Forbes, 'Sceptical Whiggism' in Skinner and Wilson (eds.), *Essays*, p. 193 and Skinner in ibid., p. 165. Ferguson's *Essay on the History of Civil Society* had appeared in 1767 and Kames's *Sketches of the History of Man* in 1774.

and sought to relate to them changes in social and political behaviour—the position of women, parental authority, the 'fluctuation of property', the power of the sovereign—in different societies at different times in history. In his chapter significantly called 'Changes produced in Government by the Progress in Arts' he provided an analytical sketch loosely equipped with historical illustrations. He concluded:

So widely different are the effects of opulence and refinement, which, at the same time that they furnish the king with a standing army, the great engine of tyranny and oppression, have also a tendency to inspire the people with notions of liberty and independence.[29]

With a 'tendency to inspire' based upon economic change, we are clearly *en route* for trends, general laws, and economic determinism. Millar went further than Smith or Hume in this direction in his major historical undertaking, *An Historical View of the English Government*, which first appeared in 1787. Although he saw it as an attempt to write a constitutional history of England,[30] it contains chapters which are the closest approximation to economic history amongst all the writings of the Scottish Enlightenment. It is evident in his chapter dealing with 'The Circumstances which promoted Commerce, Manufactures, and the Arts' in modern Europe and, particularly, in England. This is built up from a nice mixture of factual and hypothetical history. After a brief survey of the rise of European commerce in post-Barbarian times, Millar argues for a 'natural' rise of manufacturing in the following terms (my italics):

While the inhabitants of these different parts of Europe were thus advancing in navigation and commerce, *they could hardly fail* to make some progress also in manufactures. By having a vent for the rude

[29] *Origin of the Distinction of Ranks*, reprinted in W. C. Lehmann, *John Millar of Glasgow, 1735–1801* (Cambridge, 1960), p. 292.
[30] This was evident from the dedication of the original edition to Charles James Fox: '. . . it appears to me scarcely possible for any man to write a constitutional history of England . . .'.

produce of the country, *they must have had* frequent opportunities for observing that, by bestowing a little labour upon their native commodities, they could draw a much greater profit upon the exchange of them.[31]

In proceeding to encompass the growth of trade and industry in the Netherlands and England, Millar continually stresses the importance of environment and geography. From a particular base he moves to generalizations on the role of specific industries, in a manner readily recognizable in the work of later economic historians: 'the two most considerable branches of manufacture, which contribute to supply the conveniences or luxuries of any people, are the making of linen and woollen cloth'.[32] The 'three great events' which 'concurred to produce a remarkable revolution upon the state of trade and manufactures in general' were the invention of the mariner's compass, the discovery of America and of the Cape route to the East, and the Spanish destruction of the trade and industry of the southern Netherlands as a consequence of religious bigotry. And England was in the best position to take advantage of these changes, partly because of the woollen trade, its insular situation, and the like, and partly because its inhabitants were so much 'better secured in their property and protected from oppressive taxes' than elsewhere in Europe that, for all its want of improvements, 'now happily received', its constitution 'may be regarded as a system of liberty'.[33]

By now we seem to be well on our way to the Whig interpretation of English economic, as well as political, history. But there was more to come in the chapters covering the period from the accession of the Stuarts to his own day. These were put together from papers found by his executors after Millar's death in 1801 and combined with the original to

[31] John Millar, *An Historical View of the English Government* (1812 edn., 4 vols.), II, pp. 367–8.
[32] Ibid., p. 372.
[33] Ibid., pp. 378–90.

form a new four-volume edition, first published in 1803. More strikingly than in the earlier writings, these later chapters incorporated economic generalizations as well as again playing variations upon the theme of commerce and liberty. In his account, for example, of the political state of England under the Stuarts, he speaks of the growth of trade, industry, and enterprise leading men to work in 'various mechanical employments or in 'different branches of traffic' instead of as servants or retainers of the rich. Thereby were habits of mind changed:

Rising more and more to this independent situation, artificers and tradesmen were led by degrees to shake off their ancient slavish habits, to gratify their own inclinations or humours, and to indulge that love of liberty, so congenial to the mind of man, which nothing but imperious necessity is able to subdue.[34]

In sections which dealt with the period after 1688 Millar pushed the argument still further in the posthumously assembled set of essays. Their very titles are indicative, e.g.

Essay III: The Advancement of Manufactures, Commerce and the Arts, since the Reign of William III; and the Tendency of this Advancement to diffuse a Spirit of Liberty and Independence.

Essay IV: How far the Advancement of Commerce and Manufactures has contributed to the Extension and Diffusion of Knowledge and Literature.

Essay VI: The Effects of Commerce and Manufactures, and of Opulence and Civilization, upon the Morals of a People.

He built upon, quoted, and lauded the work of 'the ingenious and profound author of "The Causes of the Wealth of Nations" ' and was able already to speak of the 'universal approbation' which his idea on mercantile freedom had received.[35] After providing a brief sketch of economic develop-

---

[34] Miller, op. cit. III, pp. 101–2.
[35] Ibid., IV, p. 110.

ment, he moved on to delineate what he saw as the social, cultural, and moral consequences of such changes, drawing, in so doing, upon Smith's *Theory of Moral Sentiments*. The economic determinism is clear but the gaze was certainly not one of unblinking optimism. He saw that the increasing division of labour attendant upon the technical facts of economic advance brought narrow and stultifying lives to some, just as it brought wealth and opportunity for the pursuit of the 'elegant arts' to others.

. . . the mechanical arts admit of such minute divisions of labour, that the workmen belonging to a manufacture are each of them employed, for the most part, in a single manual operation, and have no concern in the result of their several productions. It is hardly possible that these mechanics should acquire extensive information or intelligence.
. . . It should seem, therefore, that in countries highly advanced in commerce and manufactures, the abilities and character of the labouring people, who form the great body of the nation, are liable to be affected by circumstances of an opposite nature. Their continual attention to the objects of their profession, together with the narrowness of those objects, has a powerful tendency to render them ignorant and stupid.

Although the 'progress of science and literature and of the liberal arts among the higher classes' filtering down through society, helped to disseminate knowledge and improvement, he doubted whether in Great Britain 'the artificial education thus communicated to the lower orders of the people, be sufficient to counterbalance the disadvantages of their natural situation'.[36]
It is not my purpose here to summarize the contents of Millar's writings, or indeed those of others of the Scottish Enlightenment, but rather to point to them as progenitors of what we now call economic history. Enough has surely been said not only to demonstrate that function but also to underline the width of their concern for the past. The theme of

[36] Ibid., IV, pp. 145–6.

commerce and liberty, in their hands, was far from leading to that simplistic and Panglossian *laissez-faire* of the Victorian popularizers. Whatever the validity of their economic determinism, or indeed of their economic analysis, their treatment of history sought truth by inclusion. The economic and social, political and cultural, legal and anthropological: all were part of a vision of the past which, whatever its failings, was looking beyond both the *histoire événementielle* which Lucien Febvre and Marc Bloch were to attack almost two centuries later and the narrow technicalities characteristic of so much economic history written in Britain in recent years.

3

English Reaction

... the work of Professor Millar of Glasgow, however pleasing from its liberal spirit, displays a fault too common among the philosophers of his country, that of theorizing upon an imperfect induction, and very often upon a total misapprehension of particular facts.

Henry Hallam, *View of the State of Europe during the Middle Ages* (1819)

FROM what has been said it might be supposed, in retrospect, that the early nineteenth century should have seen the burgeoning of economic history as an intellectual study in Britain, and certainly in Scotland. As is well known, nothing of the sort happened. Not for a century and more after these remarkable outpourings of the Scottish Enlightenment was such a study even begun to be recognized as suitable for scholarly enquiry. Why? 'The simple answer', it has been said, 'is that economics as understood by the classical economists of the nineteenth century was an a-historical subject, not to say an anti-historical one, while history was not conceived as being concerned with things economic'.[1] True enough as far as it goes. But, in order to understand the consequences for the pursuit of economic history in Britain, it is first necessary to examine what happened to political economy and to history in early nineteenth-century England. How did it come about that the historical element in political economy, so integral an element in Adam Smith's work, was, as Professor Hutchison has observed 'largely extruded from the orthodox

[1] N. B. Harte (ed.), *The Study of Economic History* (1971), pp. xii–xiii.

19

conception of the subject for decades to come'?[2] Likewise, how did orthodox British historiography come to avoid any serious examination of the economic elements in human experience of the past, so prominent in the work of such as John Millar?

I

The ideas of the Scottish Enlightenment on history and political economy travelled southwards by a variety of routes and were significantly changed in the process. After their earlier dissemination via the writings of Hume, and especially Smith, the agents of diffusion included the academic in the person of Dugald Stewart and the journalistic in the voice of the *Edinburgh Review*.[3] But two southbound Scots played a major part in both the dissemination and the distortion of the original role given to what had yet to be called economic history: James Mill and J. R. McCulloch.

A contemporary at Edinburgh University of Francis Jeffrey, first editor of the *Edinburgh Review*, James Mill's southward migration took him to the London-based world of journalism, authorship, and politics, and to friendship with Jeremy Bentham and David Ricardo. Those friendships, especially that with Ricardo, had much to answer for in the transmutation of eighteenth-century Scottish political economy into nineteenth-century English classical economics; and in the removal, or at any rate bowdlerization, of the role therein of the economic past. A key work in this process is Mill's *History of British India*, not for what it achieved, in praise or notoriety, but for its failings in method. Here was a topic which could have provided a singular opportunity for the integrated treatment of the past. The penetration of one country by a trading company, chartered by the rulers of an alien civilization, and

---

[2] T. W. Hutchison, *On Revolutions and Progress in Economic Knowledge* (Cambridge, 1978), p. 56.
[3] On the influence of the *Edinburgh Review* in the dissemination of the views of Smith, Millar, *et al.*, see John Clive, *Scotch Reviewers: the Edinburgh Review, 1802–15* (1957).

the subsequent transformation of the pursuit of profit into the realities of conflict and government: such an historical sequence cannot but seem, in retrospect, of course, almost ideally designed for a multi-faceted treatment of the sort at which Smith and Millar had more than hinted. It was not to be. Instead, Mill's three massive volumes when they appeared, in 1817, were not only, as Duncan Forbes has observed, a particularly 'half-baked' example of 'philosophical history',[4] replete with errors, insulting to the Hindus, and suffused with the worst sort of Benthamite arrogance; they also did nothing to explore the interrelations of the political, economic, cultural, and social aspects of two centuries of Anglo-Indian experience.

Over three-quarters of the work consisted of a narrative history of politics and conflicts among the Indian rulers, the British, and the French. This was its major, and indeed very real, achievement. A tiny part—perhaps five per cent —comprised a bare survey of the East India Company's history up to the time of the creation of the United Company in 1707, together with a skeletal account of its trading activities. Of what might then have been regarded as 'historical political economy', let alone of what might today be called economic history, there was hardly a sign. The balance of the work, mostly contained in Book II, was a sustained attack on the government, laws, customs, religions, manners, arts, and literature of Hindu civilization. It is here that Mill may seem to have used the techniques of 'philosophical' or 'conjectural' history. In reality, however, it was sham 'philosophical' history. Despite Mill's frequent use of the term 'stage of society', or variants thereof, he did not use or build upon Smith's concept of stages of economic development; he nowhere examined relationships, historical or hypothetical, between economy and society; and, indeed, he virtually ignored the chronology of the Hindu past—an extraordinary attainment for a work of history.

---

[4] Duncan Forbes, 'James Mill and India', *Cambridge Journal* v (1951), pp. 23–4.

A few examples of the technique must suffice. Contending that statements made by Hindus were inconsistent, 'the off-spring of wild and ungoverned imaginations' bearing 'the strongest marks of a rude and credulous people', Mill presented such manifestations as illustrative of 'that propensity which so universally distinguishes rude nations and forms so remarkable a characteristic of uncivilized society—of filling the ages that are past with fabulous events'.[5] Having thus, early on in Book II, disposed of Hindu statements and Hindu history, all other related phenomena could be dealt with likewise. Their taxation system was inefficient: 'an expensive mode of raising the taxes is a natural effect of a rude state of society'.[6] Hindu religion had 'gross' ideas and was 'more engaged by frivolous observances than by objects of utility': just what you could expect when 'tracing the progress of natural religion through the different stages of intellectual acquirement'.[7] Did Hindus like jugglers and 'feats of bodily agility and dexterity'? Of course, for such things were 'adapted to the taste of all men in a state of society resembling their own'.[8] Clever in the use of their craft tools? 'This sort of facility is no mark of high civilization. A dexterity in the use of its own imperfect tools is a common attribute of rude society'.[9] Sculpture, painting, music, poetry: all were more or less as they appeared 'in early stages of society'.[10] And as for metaphysics: 'the propensity to abstract speculations is . . . the natural result of the state of the human mind in a rude and ignorant age'.[11] The irony that the theoretical content of political economy might be regarded as abstract speculation seems, perhaps not surprisingly, to have passed Mill by.

The veracity or falsehood of such notions is not my concern;

[5] James Mill, *The History of British India* (3 vols., 1817), I, p. 98 and n.
[6] Ibid., I, p. 196.
[7] Ibid., pp. 210, 264, 289.
[8] Ibid., p. 315.
[9] Ibid., p. 352.
[10] Ibid., pp. 353, 356, 362–3.
[11] Ibid., p. 381.

nor even their contemptuous, intolerant, uncomprehending arrogance. What matters is that along this important channel there flowed none of the true concern with the economic past which was one of the hallmarks of the Scottish school.

Such an absence of interest in the economic past dovetailed exactly with the structure of Ricardo's own thought. He looked forward to the appearance of Mill's *History*, as a guide to whatever it was that obstructed 'man in the rational pursuit of his own happiness', and to the ways in which legislative science might bring remedies.[12] On reading it he felt his doubts dispelled about what 'legislation might do to improve society'; and expressed himself pleased with Mill's 'endeavours to refute the prevailing opinion that the Hindus are now, or ever have been, a highly civilized people'.[13] Reform was the hope and Mill's book was an aid thereto. As he wrote to him: 'Your comparison of their Government, Laws, Customs and Religion, with what *should* be the Government, Laws, Customs and Religion, of an enlightened, and highly civilized people, is exceedingly curious and instructive'[14] (my italics). But he showed no more curiosity about the historical political economy of the Hindus than he did about that of any other of the topics covered in his published correspondence or writings. Ricardo hardly ever appealed to history to make a point, to support an analytical proposition, even to illustrate an argument. As Schumpeter observed, he had no historical sense nor, indeed, 'insight into the motive powers of the social process'.[15] His ingenious mind, essentially that of a brilliant theoretician, never displayed any significant interest in the past. He applied that mind to practical problems; he allowed himself to be pushed by Mill to taking active steps, in Parliament and outside, towards positive reform in

[12] Hutchison, *Revolutions and Progress*, p. 36, quoting Ricardo to Mill, 9 November 1817.
[13] Ibid., pp. 37–8, quoting Ricardo, 18 December 1817 and 26 January 1818.
[14] P. Sraffa (ed.), *The Works and Correspondence of David Ricardo* (11 vols., Cambridge, 1951–73), VII, pp. 227–8, Ricardo to Mill, 18 December 1817.
[15] J. A. Schumpeter, *History of Economic Analysis* (1954), p. 472 and n. 2.

the economic directions to which his own ideas led; and he left an indelible mark on the structure of economic theory. But whatever he got from Mill about the role of history, it did not extend to the functions assigned to it by Smith or Millar.

McCulloch appeared to contemporaries, and has also seemed to some modern commentators, as the authentic British broadcaster of Scottish political economy.[16] He wrote more about it than anybody else; he never stopped talking and lecturing about it; and it was unquestionably he whom the conservative Peacock satirized in *Crochet Castle* in 1831 as Mr MacQuedy. Not only was he 'the modern Athenian', the interminable expounder of 'political economy, the science of sciences' but he apparently also carried the message of stage-theory by beginning everything he wrote with the words 'in the infancy of Society ... '.[17] Admittedly, McCulloch was more interested in the economic past than any of his fellow-expounders of political economy; and the subsequent development of economic history as an academic subject in Britain has a debt to McCulloch for his work in assembling historical tracts and statistics. But, for him, the past had one highly specialized use: it was there to demonstrate the fallaciousness of past economic ideas and policies. Thereby it gave support to current political economy, to what were presented as the unquestionable truths of a particular sort of economic theory and a particular set of policy recommendations. He was undoubtedly, as has been said, 'a writer very much in the Scottish tradition'; and there were elements of the inductive method in his approach.[18] Yet, there are important differences between him and the luminaries of that tradition.

Some of these differences are probably no more than the result of an added and superabundant confidence, a degree of dogmatic certainty which appals by the repetition of assertions, almost word for word, in article after article, book after

[16] See e.g. D. P. O'Brien, *J. R. McCulloch: A Study in Classical Economics* (1970).

[17] T. L. Peacock, *Crotchet Castle* (1831) in *Works* (ed. D. Garnett, 2 vols., 1963), II, pp. 660, 686.

[18] O'Brien, *McCulloch*, pp. 97–8.

book. They testify to the contrast between thought and popularization, separated by sixty and more years. Within that contrast, however, there is contained the more important omission of matters which were of central concern to Smith and, especially, to Millar: the nature and sequence of economic growth, the divergent effects of the pursuit of 'opulence', the regard for the complex interaction between politics, society, and commerce. What McCulloch offered in his historical works may be seen in, for example, the *Statistical Account of the British Empire.*[19] Here, along with a mass of geographical information, was a conventional Whiggish account of the political history of England, Scotland, and Ireland, a further mass of information on current legal and constitutional matters, and a history of British commerce and manufactures in much greater detail than had been provided hitherto. These various parts were all separately treated.

The part which might seem most to approximate to what would now be called economic history consisted of two main elements. One was a very substantial supply of factual data, quantitative and otherwise. In providing this, the Scottish tradition which McCulloch drew upon was not that of Hume, Smith, Millar, or Ferguson but that of the chroniclers Adam Anderson and David Macpherson. Both were Scots who, like McCulloch, emigrated southwards; both, like McCulloch and unlike Smith, were essentially fact-grubbers rather than original thinkers in their own right. Anderson's *Historical and Chronological Deduction of the Origins of Commerce . . . containing an History of the great Commercial Interests of the British Empire* appeared in two volumes in 1764 and offered a series of chronologies from the fall of the Roman Empire onwards. It is simply a compilation of data, not primarily quantitative, and unaccompanied by any analysis, mercantilist or otherwise. Indeed, Anderson was anxious to present it as an impartial offering. He acknowledged his indebtedness to William Fleetwood's *Chronicon Preciosum*—that pioneer work in the

[19] (2 vols., 1837).

collecting of historical prices, which had appeared in 1707— and to such late seventeenth-century writers as Petty, Child, and Graunt. But he evidently sought to insure himself against possible accusations of bias; he remarked of Evelyn's *Navigation and Commerce* that it tended to 'illustrate rather in the Manner of Harangue than of History'.[20] Some forty years later, Macpherson presented his *Annals of Commerce* as an improved and updated version of Anderson's work which he accused of having 'innumerable errors and omissions'.[21] Exactly the same type of chronicle as Anderson's, it extended the coverage to 1801 and provided more statistical information. Macpherson's introductory and passing comments also had a more evidently Whiggish flavour with touches of Enlightenment phraseology:

Wherever commerce has flourished, the people have enjoyed general plenty and happiness; civilization, urbanity and a comparatively well-ordered government, securing the liberty and prosperity of the subject, have been its constant attendants.[22]

A characteristic addition was a nice footnote comment, incorporating suitably post-Smithian views, to Anderson's version of the abortive 1713 Anglo-French commercial Treaty of Utrecht.[23] With Macpherson's criticism of Anderson that some of the latter's comments had been 'dictated by the narrow-spirited jealousy of commerce, which in his time passed for patriotism',[24] we are clearly *en route* for McCulloch.

The second element in McCulloch's presentation of the economic past consists simply of a long series of deprecating comments, ridiculing every sort of enactment which could be seen as impeding the free movement of market forces, the total liberty of the individual to pursue economic ends, or the

---

[20] A. Anderson, *Origins of Commerce* (2 vols., 1764), I, p. v.
[21] D. Macpherson, *Annals of Commerce* (4 vols., 1805), I, p. iv.
[22] Ibid., p. iii.
[23] Ibid., III, p. 30.
[24] Ibid., I, p. v.

security and free disposal of property. It is here, of course, that the debt to the other Scottish tradition is more apparent; and, indeed, McCulloch in his *Dictionary of Commerce*,[25] for example, quotes from Hume, Smith, Ferguson, and others. The tone, however, is notably different, with confident assertion replacing reasoned argument. 'All regulations affecting the freedom of commerce, or of any branch of industry', he firmly announced, 'are either useless or pernicious'.[26] As for the balance of trade: 'it is difficult to estimate the mischief which the absurd notions relative to the balance of trade have occasioned in almost every commercial country'.[27] Always willing to state and restate the theory upon which such observations were based, McCulloch never showed any disposition to analyse the historical evidence for such implicitly counterfactual statements. Instead, just as in his introductions to the early economic tracts which he republished he awarded praise or blame for the correctness or otherwise of the theories they supposedly embodied, so, in his own writings, acts of historical economic policy were similarly reported on by this inveterate pedagogue of political economy.[28] Consequently, his use of the economic past, wherever it is to be found—in the *Dictionary*, the *Discourse on the Rise, Progress . . . of Political Economy*, or even the *Principles*—is always polemical.[29] Because of the historical information on economic matters which he collected and published, and because of the sheer repetitive bulk of his writings thereon, he has to be seen as attendant upon the birth of economic history in Britain. But his legacy was a combination of economic antiquarianism and the unquestioning acceptance of a particular economic theory; nor did he bequeath any contribution to the integrated examination

---

[25] *A Dictionary, Practical, Theoretical and Historical of Commerce and Commercial Navigation* (1832).

[26] McCulloch, *Dictionary*, p. 352.

[27] Ibid., p. 55.

[28] See, e.g., his introductory comments in *Early Tracts*, pp. iii–xv.

[29] See, e.g., *Discourse on the Rise, Progress, Peculiar Objects and Importance of Political Economy* (1824), pp. 24–40.

of the economic, social, and political past. Thus, in these ways, far from continuing the tradition of the Scottish Enlightenment, McCulloch helped to debase and undermine it.

So, by the mid-nineteenth century, the combined efforts of Mill, Ricardo, and McCulloch had gone far to remove the historical elements from the formulation of economic theory. History had been relegated to the subsidiary role of providing illustrations of what were confidently regarded as the ignorance and foolishness of past attempts by governments to influence the economy.

II

Meanwhile, British historiography had been going its own way, in happy separation from the economic past. 'Conjectual history' made no significant headway south of the border; Millar's attempts at the integration of the political, the social, and the economic were not developed. Some historians announced their intention to trace such interactions but few achieved anything.[30] The work of Millar's fellow Scot, George Brodie, whose *History of the British Empire* appeared in 1822, clearly showed the influence of Scottish Enlightenment philosophy in its introductory chapters on 'the Progress of Society' in England.[31] Indeed, they contained some unusual and perceptive observations on Tudor policy concerning enclosures. Though generally following Smithian lines, they also ran to an appendix questioning some of Adam Smith's views on the non-desirability of protection and offering an alternative set of policy recommendations.[32] After these essentially introductory observations, however, the bulk of the work was entirely devoted to British political history from the end of Elizabeth's

[30] For some examples see T. P. Peardon, *The Transition in English Historical Writing, 1760–1830* (New York, 1933), pp. 34–5, 62–3; and J. W. Burrow, *A Liberal Descent* (Cambridge, 1981), pp. 21–35.
[31] George Brodie, *A History of the British Empire* (4 vols., Edinburgh, 1822).
[32] Ibid., I, pp. 25 ff. and Note B.

reign to the Restoration, and was especially concerned to attack Hume's views on the Tudors and Stuarts.

Neither stages of economic growth nor the progress of civil society had much appeal for the generation of English historians who were to embody high-Victorian orthodoxy. By various routes and in various manifestations, they became and remained obsessed by what was seen as the political and constitutional uniqueness of Britain. The old sort of rhetoric about the ancient liberties of England, about free Anglo-Saxons, the glories of Magna Carta, and the 'antiquity and independence of the House of Commons'[33] underwent complex refinements in interpretation as scholarly work on original documents advanced. The crudities of post-revolutionary Whig and Tory history gave way to an updated Whig interpretation of English history in both its Butterfieldean and its literal meaning. Its apex, in scholarly terms, is to be found in that view of the British past enshrined in the writings of a succession of historians from Hallam through Stubbs and Freeman to Trevelyan. Yet, in all this, it is doubtful whether the 'scientific Whiggism', to use Duncan Forbes' phrase, of Smith and Millar had any significant effect; and certainly the economic determinism with which both approached the relations between commerce and liberty had no attractions for the new orthodoxy despite a consciousness of the triumphant advance of the British economy.[34]

Hallam's *Constitutional History of England*—the appearance of which, in 1827, approximately coincided with McCulloch's appointment to the Chair of Political Economy at the new University of London—marked a first highlight in this sort of history. Learned and lofty, measured and dignified, it was also, as Dr Burrow has observed, 'legalistic, constitutionalist and insular'.[35] Despite the inclusion in his earlier (1819) *View*

---

[33] H. Butterfield, *The Englishman and his History* (Cambridge, 1944), p. 70.

[34] Duncan Forbes, ' "Scientific" Whiggism: Adam Smith and John Millar', *Cambridge Journal* VII (1954), pp. 643–70; M. Ignatieff, 'John Millar and Individualism' in I. Hont and M. Ignatieff (eds.), *Wealth and Virtue* (Cambridge, 1983), p. 326.

[35] Burrow, *Liberal Descent*, p. 30.

of the State of Europe during the Middle Ages of what he called a 'slight survey of œconomical history',[36] Hallam's ultimate concern with such aspects of the past was to present them as merely incidental aids to his vision of the 'long and uninterruptedly increasing prosperity of England as the most beautiful phenomenon in the history of mankind'.[37] He made it clear, moreover, that he saw that prosperity as having been achieved by England entirely as a consequence of 'the spirit of its laws, from which through various means, the characteristic independence and industriousness of our nation have been derived'.[38] Hence, intellectual curiosity should be directed at our constitution and its history. And as for Millar and other such Scots:

the work of Professor Millar of Glasgow, however pleasing from its liberal spirit, displays a fault too common among the philosophers of his country, that of theorizing upon an imperfect induction, and very often upon a total misapprehension of particular facts.[39]

With Macaulay, the advance of the new orthodoxy achieved its first surge of popularity. For, to this Whig picture of beautiful insular advance, he brought both a romantic and imaginative way of thought (influenced by the writings of Walter Scott) and an heroic (not to say fruity) literary style. To this heady mixture were also added some traces of Scottish Enlightenment political economy in its more optimistic and less 'scientific' form. In the celebrated third chapter of his *History*, Macaulay, it has been said, 'made a bid to incorporate the industrial revolution into the Whig interpretation of history'.[40] But where, one might reasonably ask, is the industrial revolution in that chapter? Where is power-driven machinery and where the factory? Despite his attempts to

[36] H. Hallam, *View of the State of Europe during the Middle Ages* (2nd edn., 3 vols., 1819), III, p. 445.
[37] Ibid., II, p. 374.
[38] Ibid., p. 375.
[39] Ibid., I, p. xi.
[40] Burrow, *Liberal Descent*, p. 65.

provide contrasts between the England of 1685 and the indus-
trializing England of his own day, rather more space is spent
on the growth of Cheltenham, Bath, and Tunbridge Wells
than on coal and iron; and very much more on the prosperity
and cultural attainments of the gentry and clergy than on the
expansion of commerce and industry. If the balance of topics
reflected the balance of interests of his likely readers, so they
naturally mirrored the cast of Macaulay's mind. For all his
occasional lip-service to the 'progress of society', he was not at
home with Smith or Millar; nor was he in any serious way a
systematic social thinker.[41] The third chapter is little more
than an extended application, in descriptive historical terms,
of what he had written in 1830 in his refutation of Robert
Southey's arch-Tory, anti-industrialist glorification of the past
at the expense of the present.[42] The result has all of
McCulloch's brash optimism but none of Millar's questioning. It was all very well for Macaulay to write that 'History
was too much occupied with courts and camps to spare a time
for the hut of the peasant or the garret of the mechanic'.[43] But,
in reality, a line or two represented his idea of the proportion
to be devoted to such matters, just as huts and garrets typified
for him the intellectual as well as the social status of industrial
topics. The third chapter, as Dr Burrow has suggested,
marked a defeat 'for industry and the idea of progress in their
long failure to establish a rapport with . . . the English literary
mind'.[44] A century after that third chapter was written, not
only the English literary mind but also the orthodox English
historical mind still had little time for industry and still less for
economic growth. Macaulay has much to answer for in sus-
taining those deficiencies. He was a narrative historian with a
superb romantic style which had a lasting public appeal; and

[41] J. Clive, *Thomas Babington Macaulay: The Shaping of an Historian* (1973), pp. 118–19.
[42] 'Southey's Colloquies', *Edinburgh Review* (January 1830), reprinted in T. B. Macaulay, *Critical and Historical Essays* (Everyman edn., 2 vols., 1967), II, pp. 187–224.
[43] T. B. Macaulay, *History of England* (1889 edn., 2 vols.), I, p. 202.
[44] Burrow, *Liberal Descent*, p. 65. As he has further remarked, the *History* as a whole,
despite the famous third chapter, 'remains obstinately political' (p. 66).

he did more than anyone else to define the nature of popular history for several generations of Britons.

His vision of the English past from the twelfth century to the nineteenth is best summed up in a passage from an essay he wrote in 1835. In the course of these seven centuries, a

wretched and degraded race have become the greatest and most highly civilised people that ever the world saw, have spread their dominion over every quarter of the globe, have scattered the seeds of mighty empires and republics over vast continents of which no dim intimation had ever reached Ptolemy or Strabo, have created a maritime power which would annihilate in a quarter of an hour the navies of Tyre, Athens, Carthage, Venice, and Genoa together, have carried the science of healing, the means of locomotion and corres- pondence, every mechanical art, every manufacture, everything that promotes the convenience of life, to a perfection which our ancestors would have thought magical, have produced a literature which may boast of works not inferior to the noblest which Greece has bequeathed to us, have discovered the laws which regulate the motions of the heavenly bodies, have speculated with exquisite subtilty on the operations of the human mind, have been the acknowledged leaders of the human race in the career of political improvement.[45]

He offered this as a testimony to his conviction that the history of England was 'emphatically the history of progress'. This, however, is not 'the progress of society' as Smith or Millar knew it. It is rodomontade. It is also indistinguishable in its tone from such statements as this:

The errors with which Political Economy was formerly infected have now nearly disappeared, and a very few observations will suffice to show that it really admits of as much certainty in its conclusions as any Science founded on fact and experiment can possibly do.

Thus McCulloch in 1824 and 1863 alike.[46] The Scottish

---

[45] 'Sir James Mackintosh', *Edinburgh Review*, (July 1835), repr. in *Essays*, I, p. 292.
[46] *Discourse*, quoted in Hutchison, *Revolutions and Progress*, p. 219 and n. 12. Professor Hutchison notes that McCulloch was content to reprint in 1863 such statements as this which he had made in the first ed. of 1824.

Enlightenment had been bowdlerized. History and political economy were divorced. In their separate states, they were equally convinced, complacent, and triumphant.

III

To attempt to explain the reasons for the separation and its particular timing would demand investigation quite outside the scope of this work. Suffice to look at some possibly relevant considerations.

English historians' nationalist obsession with liberty and the constitution was obviously given a powerful fillip by the quite extraneous happenings of revolutionary Europe. For many people in England the successive events of 1789, 1830, and 1848, however they may have inspired some and frightened others, did not fail to evoke support for a presentation of the island story, be it in learned or popular terms, as one of liberty triumphant by constitutional means. If there was indeed a parallel growth in the nation's commerce, industry, and wealth, there could have been no doubt, in the minds of presenters and readers alike, about the direction in which causality flowed. For the overwhelming majority of those brought up in the classical liberal education of the day, it would have been inconceivable that it might have flowed from the lowly 'mechanic arts' to the polity. The proper business of history, whether or not it was still seen as philosophy teaching by example, was with rulers and ruling groups, with men and the manipulation of power by the law or by conflict. Though merchants might grow into patricians, the techniques of trade were no more the stuff of patrician education than were the techniques of cotton spinning or coal mining.

There were also, of course, more prosaic reasons for the neglect by historians of the economic past. Evidence of the doings of ordinary men and women in their pursuit of production, consumption, and profit, as well as of the resulting distribution of wealth, was much harder to obtain than was that of policy and power enshrined in the records of state. It still is. It was a complaint quite often voiced, though whether as genuine lament or rather as pretext for moving on to the narrative of matters of greater moment and esteem, it is hard to say. However, even if the more readily available material was gathered in, a different problem had still to be faced. How was the resulting text to be fitted in to the structure of the intended historical treatise? In short, where to put it?

The scattering of a few fragments of social and economic comment in text or footnotes can be found in Gibbon, Voltaire, or Bolingbroke. It cannot, for example, have been difficult for Bolingbroke to place his comments on the increase in the property of the Commons, the creation of funds, the multiplication of taxes, or the rise of the monied interest, at suitable points in his letters and reflections on history.[47] But, as Dugald Stewart observed, if one wished to 'connect with the view of political transactions, an examination of their effects on the manners and condition of mankind, and to blend the lights of philosophy with the appropriate beauties of historical composition', then more serious problems arose. The historian had to choose between 'the alternative either of interrupting unseasonably the chain of events, or, by interweaving disquisition and narrative together, of sacrificing clearness to brevity'.[48] As already noted, Hume saw himself as necessarily 'departing from the historical style' when he paused to write about matters economic and social.[49] Macaulay's third chapter made a very obvious and stylistically unsatisfactory break in his narrative at the moment when 'the crown passed from Charles the Second to his brother'; and he excused the result as 'a description, composed from scanty and dispersed matters, [which] must neces-

---

[47] Lord Bolingbroke, *Historical Writings* (ed. I. Kramnick, Chicago, 1972), pp. 20–1, 232, etc.
[48] Dugald Stewart, *Account of the Life and Writings of William Robertson, D.D., F.R.S.E.* (2nd edn., 1802), p. 139.
[49] Above, p. 9.

sarily be very imperfect'.[50] So long as history meant the narrative of power, any examination of the relationship of that power to economy and society was an intruder, and worthy of only marginal accommodation.

If, for these diverse reasons, English historians were thus content to ignore or trivialize the economic past in pursuit of a narrative of insular constitutional achievement, the political economists found other aids to their own abandonment of that historical context in which Smith had lodged their subject. For Mill, Ricardo, and McCulloch, political economy was a new science to deal with new problems, to light the way to still greater national wealth, to inform legislatures of the path to progress. Assuredly not the *scienza nuova* of Vico, but certainly an agent for Benthamite reform. In the half-century separating the publication of the *Wealth of Nations* and, say, the third edition of James Mill's *Principles of Political Economy* (1826), the first phases of the industrial revolution had done more than generate new wealth. They had galvanized pressure groups keen to gain access to markets ringed by tariffs or to be rid of legislation controlling wages or prices. They had created 'the machinery question' and the social dilemma of the handloom weavers. In combination with population growth and the Napoleonic wars, they had presented the need for reform in the fields of finance and banking, as well as in those of the corn laws. To all and more, the new political economy claimed to have answers—new, sharp, bright scientific answers.

Not everyone believed in those answers. The economic policy of the 1820s was, indeed, often 'pragmatically rather than theoretically motivated'.[51] The social problems generated by the impact of machinery and the growth of towns stimulated opposition—moral or theoretical, idealistic Utopian or highest of Tory—to the dogmatism of the pundits.[52] Political economy did not always speak with a

[50] *History*, i, pp. 136–7.
[51] Boyd Hilton, *Corn, Cash, Commerce* (Oxford, 1977), p. 70.
[52] See Maxine Berg, *The Machinery Question and the Making of Political Economy* (Cambridge, 1980).

single voice. Industrial or commercial pressure groups had conflicting interests and by no means all espoused free trade. Nevertheless, a new body of vigorously enunciated opinion was in the air, publicized and popularized; and new experts were consulted by those who ruled the country. Their views were not ignored; and, in the formulation and enunciation of the dominant opinion, history played no significant role. The economic past was marshalled merely to show the errors of the past. It was only the heterodox opponents of the dominant voice who appealed to history. For the orthodox, 'economicall history' had nothing positive to say. Recovery after the post-war depression and expansion into the triumphant mid-century boom seemed to make the merits of free trade and *laissez-faire* self-evident, to justify the deductive approach, and to set the seal of approval on what had become classical political economy. As Nassau Senior explained to a Frenchman just after the Great Exhibition of 1851, the prosperity of Britain was 'a triumph of theory. We are governed by philosophers and political economists'.[53]

[53] Nassau Senior, *Conversations with M. Thiers, M. Guizot and other Distinguished Persons during the Second Empire* (1878), vol. I, p. 169, quoted in A. Gerschenkron, 'History of Economic Doctrines and Economic History', Papers and Proceedings of the American Economic Association, *American Economic Review* (May 1969), pp. 370–85.

4

Rebels, Outsiders, and Economic Historians

The integration of history with analysis and theory, so superbly and uniquely achieved in Adam Smith's work was shattered . . . Economic history was left largely to rebels and outsiders.

T. W. Hutchison, *On Revolutions and Progress in Economic Knowledge* (1978)[1]

BETWEEN approximately 1880 and 1910, the first major steps were taken by which economic history came to be recognized as a subject suitable for study in British universities. A scatter of appointments were made, culminating in the first chair in economic history in Britain. Some notable (and some less notable) textbooks and monographs made their appearance. A growing general interest in the subject became evident in various quarters outside the universities; and it began to find a place in the examinations of some professional bodies. These early years of a new focus of intellectual endeavour have been chronicled from time to time and there is no point in recapitulating the story here.[2] Suffice very briefly to set out certain landmarks in order to aid subsequent consideration of those features which seem crucial in shaping the course and fate of the subject in years to come.

---

[1] Hutchison, *Revolutions and Progress*, pp. 54–5.
[2] The most comprehensive and detailed account, complete with bibliography, is the editor's introduction, 'The Making of Economic History' in Harte (ed.), *Study*, pp. xi–xxxix, which should be supplemented by T. C. Barker, 'The Beginnings of the Economic History Society', *Econ. Hist. Rev.* 2nd Ser. xxx (1977), pp. 1–19. The following section draws heavily on Mr Harte's admirable survey.

I

In the course of the 1880s, lectures in economic history were being given at both Oxford and Cambridge and books prepared or published. At Oxford, J. E. Thorold Rogers, during his second tenure of the Drummond Chair of Political Economy and also as a lecturer at Worcester College, was lecturing on the subject and in 1822 and 1887 brought out volumes III–VI of his massive *History of Agriculture and Prices* (the first two volumes appeared in 1866 and the last two, posthumously, in 1902).[3] Arnold Toynbee's lectures attracted much attention and, after his early death, were brought together and published as *Lectures on the Industrial Revolution* (1884). A year later William Ashley published the first volume of his *Introduction to English Economic History and Theory*, the second volume appearing in 1893. Meanwhile, in Cambridge, William Cunningham was providing lectures on economic history for the recently founded History Tripos (it started in 1873 and Economic History became a separate paper in 1885 after having, as in Oxford, been joined with Political Economy). In 1882 he published his *Growth of English Industry and Commerce* which proved to be merely the first of a three-volume epic that had reached a fifth edition by 1910.[4] In 1892 Ashley went to Harvard University to become the first Professor of Economic History in the English-speaking world—returning to England in 1901 to become Professor of Commerce at Birmingham University—and W. A. S. Hewins published his *English Trade and Finance mainly in the Seventeenth Century*. In 1895 Hewins became the first Director of the newly formed London School of Economics and Political Science and set about ensuring that economic history was an integral part of the curriculum. Over the next few years, Hewins, Cunningham, and others taught economic history at LSE, which in 1910 became part of the University of London. Amongst those

---

[3] Also *Six Centuries of Work and Wages* (1884).

[4] Vol. I (1882) reached its fifth edition in 1910; vol. II came out in two parts in 1892 and had reached a fourth edition by 1907.

others were Ashley, Hubert Hall, Ellen MacArthur, and Lilian Tomm (later Mrs Lilian Knowles), who in 1904 was appointed Lecturer in Economic History at LSE. This was the first full-time university post in the subject in Britain. Other such economic history lectureships followed in quick succession: H. O. Meredith at Manchester University in 1905, L. L. Price at Oxford in 1907, George Unwin (whose *Industrial Organization in the Sixteenth and Seventeenth Centuries* had appeared in 1904) at Edinburgh in 1908, R. L. Jones at Belfast in 1910. This sequence of dawning university recognition was capped by the appointment of Unwin to the first British chair in economic history, at Manchester in 1910 and of Lilian Knowles to the second, at LSE, in 1921.

Meanwhile, the subject had been making its mark outside. The University Extension movement and, after 1903, the Workers Education Association, found economic history especially appropriate to their needs. A number of the economic historians already mentioned were active lecturers for these organizations at one time or another. Growing appeal also stimulated a flow of textbooks. H. de B. Gibbins, *Industrial History of England* (1890) and Townsend Warner, *Landmarks in English Industrial History* (1899) both sold very well and were soon joined by L. L. Price, *Short History of English Commerce and Industry* (1900) and H. O. Meredith, *Outline of the Economic History of England* (1908).

So much for the barest of bare factual outlines, a mere list of appointments and publications. But how had they emerged after that earlier divorce between history and political economy? And what were the features attending birth, youth, and adolescence which were later to mark the mature subject?

II

It needs to be stressed at the outset that what happened within 'political economy', as it grew into 'economics' during the second half of the nineteenth century, proceeded independently of the emergence of economic history as a separate subject. The publication in 1848 of John Stuart Mill's *Principles of Political Economy*, which ran through numerous editions in the next fifty years, set the seal on a slightly modified form of Ricardian economics. Less extreme in his views than his father, J. S. Mill allowed that history and other sources of empirical evidence might be useful for verifying theories, but political economy remained for him essentially an abstract science.[5] It formulated law, operated independently of other sorts of social enquiry, and had provided itself with an intellectual forum in the shape of the Political Economy Club.

Whether or not the important changes in method introduced into its study in the 1870s and 1880s deserved the title of 'the marginal revolution', for the growing contemporary study of economic history the significance of those changes was essentially negative. The absorption into the body of economic theory of the ideas associated with W. S. Jevons in Britain, with Carl Menger in Austria, and with Léon Walras in France certainly brought a great access of both precision and flexibility. The essence of the change was an extensive application to economic ideas of the differential calculus. Out went classical value theory and the wages-fund; in came marginal cost and marginal productivity. The concepts were basically mathematical; and the standard form of textbook exposition came, in time, to be the sequence of logical argument, interspersed with geometry, and capped by a mathematical appendix, familiar to all twentieth-century students of economics. The transformation of political economy into economics had been accomplished. But the new flower had blossomed on old stock; it was a graft not a new species. Whatever the arguments about a 'revolution', there is no argument that the result was 'neo-classical'. In Britain it was triumphantly embodied in Alfred Marshall's *Principles of Economics* of 1890. It had run to eight editions by 1920, was reprinted many times

[5] Hutchison, *Revolutions and Progress*, pp. 61–4; P. Deane, *The Evolution of Economic Ideas* (Cambridge, 1978), p. 89.

thereafter, and long remained a standard work. In its aim stated in the Preface to the first edition, 'to present a modern version of old doctrines with the aid of new work', it was highly successful. The tone was moderate, the embrace catholic (especially in the attention which Marshall paid to history), and 'the laws of economics' were no longer presented as immutable truths but as 'statements of tendencies expressed in the indicative mood, and not ethical precepts in the imperative'.[6]

Despite these qualifications and despite Marshall's own considerable historical knowledge and interests—made evident in his *Industry and Trade* (1919)—it represented a defeat for the historicist school of critics. It was intended to. For Marshall had a wholly different view of the proper relationship between history and economics. The historicists saw history as a shaper of economic theory; Marshall presented economic theory as crucial for the full understanding of history. 'Social science' and more specifically, economics, was to be the basis for a 'reasoned history of man'. Economic reasoning was to provide the explanatory tools; economic history was merely one contributor to that greater reasoned history of man.[7] The skilful moderation of Marshall's approach ensured that it was victory by rejuvenation, innovation, and the inclusive embrace. Nevertheless, it was the school of the historicists, not that of the new neo-classical economics, which initially left its mark upon and, indeed, helped to stimulate the emergence of the pioneer economic historians. The German historians, especially Wilhelm Roscher and, later, Gustav Schmoller, seem in retrospect to personify one important continental European criticism of the insular English classical political economy. Although this particular aspect of German intellectual life provided an evident influence—if only because

[6] Marshall, *Principles* (8th edn., 1920), Preface to the first edition, pp. v and vi.
[7] See A. C. Pigou (ed.), *Memorials of Alfred Marshall* (1925), pp. 299–300. For a valuable and extended discussion of Marshall's views on history and economics see S. Collini, D. Winch, and J. Burrow, *That Noble Science of Politics* (Cambridge, 1983), pp. 311–37.

Cunningham, Ashley, and, in a quite different way, Unwin were all affected by their works—there was a continuing native British historical challenge to Ricardian economics. This line of protest demands attention because it offers an internal clue to the oppositional stance of economic historiography in Britain.

Among the earliest critics of Ricardian abstraction who came to make appeals to empirical evidence, in protest, was Malthus. Both in his famous *Essay on Population* and his *Principles of Political Economy*, he combined abstract argument and empirical evidence to a far greater extent than did Ricardo. Or, to be more exact, he came to do so in successive editions of his work, notably in the *Essay on Population*. The 1798 edition is largely an exercise in reasoning cast in a characteristic 'Enlightenment' mould of stages of society. By the time the *Essay* had reached its sixth edition of 1826, it had grown so substantial an accretion of historical and statistical evidence that it had become virtually a different book. In his *Principles*, too, he sometimes delved into history, as, for example, in his discussion of the relations between population and prices in sixteenth-century England.[8] And he did, after all, occupy the Professorship of History and Political Economy at the East India College, Haileybury. So, although Malthus seems not to have made a very strong impact in the economists' own debate (Schumpeter dismissed him as 'not a good controversialist'),[9] he deserves an honoured place amongst the progenitors of the study of the economic and social past in Britain. And he earns that place by virtue not only of methodology but of his concern for morality and social improvement: his view that political economy resembled more 'the science of morals and politics than . . . that of mathematics'[10] would have commended itself as little to neo-classical economists or latter-day cliometricians as it did to his contemporaries of the school of

[8] T. R. Malthus, *Principles of Political Economy* (2nd edn., 1836; repr. Oxford, 1951), pp. 252–6.
[9] Schumpeter, *History*, p. 481.
[10] Malthus, *Principles*, p. 1.

Ricardo. But in sentiment it is almost pure Tawney, even though the conclusions of the two men would have been very different.

Richard Jones, Malthus's successor at Haileybury and also Professor of Political Economy at King's College, London, identified himself more clearly with the nineteenth-century inductionist school. He stressed the need to study 'the economy of nations in the past and present story of the world at large'; presented history and statistics as the only sources from which 'the teacher of political economy' could derive his material; and emphasized the connection between political economy and 'the political elements out of which governments are formed'.[11] His impact was not, however, very substantial. His written works were few and slight; his own historical research limited.[12] He did not much deflect the onward march of political economy towards neo-classical economics.

If, nevertheless, he struck a responsive chord in the minds of those moving towards the study of economic history, still more so did Cliffe Leslie, who overshadows Jones in the genealogy of British economic historians. In his *Essays in Political and Moral Philosophy*, which appeared in 1879, Leslie revealed the influence both of Sir Henry Maine and of the German historical school, as well as drawing upon the writers of the Scottish Enlightenment. Leslie, like his contemporary and fellow advocate of the historical approach to political economy, J. K. Ingram, was a product of Trinity College, Dublin. He vigorously attacked the facile dogmatism of popularized orthodox political economy; called for a return to the historical elements in Smith's works; and announced roundly that 'no branch of philosophical doctrine . . . can be fairly investigated or apprehended apart from its history'.[13] The

[11] William Whewell (ed.), *Literary Remains consisting of Lectures and Tracts on Political Economy of the late Rev. Richard Jones* (1859), pp. 560, 570, 574.

[12] Although he continued to lecture at Haileybury, much of his time was given to advisory and administrative activities in connection with the commutation of tithes, on which he became a recognized authority (see Whewell, pp. xxvii–xxxviii).

[13] *Essays in Political and Moral Philosophy*, p. 149.

influence of Maine's studies of historical jurisprudence bore upon Leslie when he was reading for the bar in London (though Professor of Jurisprudence and Political Economy at Queen's College, Belfast, he normally lived in London) and antedated the influence of the German historicists.[14] He was, however, one of the first economists to stress their importance, notably in an article in the *Fortnightly Review*, in 1875, which described and analysed the 'two different conceptions of political economy [which] now divide economists throughout Europe . . . the English and the German'.[15] Had Leslie not died relatively young and had he not apparently lost the manuscript of a nearly completed economic history of England,[16] he might have figured as one of the country's pioneer economic historians. As it was, the union of the native line of opposition to orthodox economics with that of the German historical school was made manifest in Ashley and Cunningham.

After gaining first-class honours in history at Oxford, and being influenced there by Toynbee, Ashley studied with Schmoller in Berlin. His *Introduction to English Economic History and Theory* is a lucid and learned disquisition on the economic life of medieval England up to the mid-sixteenth century. The 'theory' of the title comprises a study of Canonist doctrine, views on the 'just price', medieval attitudes to economic activity as revealed in legislation, and similar exemplifications to support the comment, firmly stated in his Preface, that 'modern economic theories . . . are not universally true'[17] With these words of 1888, Ashley was clearly tilting at orthodox political economy and speaking up for the historical economists. By the time he came to give his inaugural lecture

---

[14] See the important article on Leslie by Gerard M. Koot, 'T. E. Cliffe Leslie, Irish Social Reform, and the Origins of the English Historical School of Economics', *History of Political Economy* VII (1975), pp. 312–36.

[15] Reprinted in his *Essays*, p. 167.

[16] Koot, 'Cliffe Leslie', p. 315. Leslie died in 1882 at the age of 55.

[17] W. Ashley, *Introduction to Economic History and Theory* (vol. I, 1888; vol. II, 1893. 4th edn., 1913) I, p. xi.

at Harvard, in 1893, the tone had been modified and he acknowledged that the hope for an historical economics had not been realized. What had happened, instead, was the birth of economic history as an academic subject in British universities. Incidentally, Ashley's bibliographical pages brought to the attention of British students and scholars the significant number of works by German scholars, not only on social and economic history in general, but specifically on England.

Cunningham, though also impressed by the Germans, particularly Roscher, belonged rather more to the native line of protest. But Cunningham and Ashley together, as L. L. Price put it in 1900, 'created Economic History for English students'.[18] Some ten years older than Ashley, Cunningham was a highly successful product of the Cambridge Moral Sciences Tripos, an energetic and combative historian, College lecturer and Fellow of Trinity, a cleric who had much to say from the pulpit of Great St Mary's, and a prolific writer.[19] His *magnum opus, The Growth of English Industry and Commerce*, is essentially the work of a political historian of a conservative disposition who happened to be fascinated by economic phenomena. Its prime focus of interest is the activity of government in the social and economic sphere. It is not about 'theory' in the sense that Ashley uses the word. 'Economic history', wrote Cunningham, 'is not so much the study of a special class of facts as the study of all the facts of a nation's history from a special point of view'.[20] He too tilted against Mill and orthodox political economy, and, of course, against Marshall. His combat with Marshall is well-documented and its consequences for the burgeoning profession of economics in Britain

[18] Quoted Harte (ed.), *Study*, p. xxvi.

[19] Cunningham at Cambridge was later recalled by Trevelyan observing that when 'his heavy, bearded figure moved majestically across the Great Court [of Trinity College] under the shadow of his huge Archdeacon's hat, he seemed to have walked into our world out of Trollope's Barchester'. G. M. Trevelyan, *An Autobiography and Other Essays* (1949), p. 22.

[20] *The Growth of English Industry and Commerce*, vol. 1 (5th edn., 1910), p. 8.

have been properly emphasized.[21] 'The conflict between Marshall and Cunningham', it has been said, 'was over the future of economics: the future of economic history was scarcely, if at all, involved'.[22] But it was involved, not consciously, perhaps, but certainly in its unforeseen results. For it helped—along with the historicist affiliations of Ashley—to ensure that, in the longer run, economic history in Britain was seen by economists as peripheral to their interests; that some degree of mutual antagonism developed between the practitioners of the two subjects; and that, although in its early years it was nurtured more by history faculties than by economics, it later tended to become a separated entity, neither quite economic fish nor historic fowl.

A variety of incidents and echoes bear witness to the significance for economic history of this early split between Marshall and Cunningham. As the latter had distinguished himself in moral philosophy, so had the former in mathematics. For Marshall, the appropriate expression of the ideal in economics was 'scientific' rather than 'scholarly'; and 'literary' was effectively a term of derogation.[23] Such contrasting expressions amongst economists and historians are almost as evident today as then. His long-running conflict with Henry Sidgwick, creator and custodian of the Moral Sciences Tripos, led Marshall to talk of 'the oppression and suppression of economics by the incubus of Moral Sciences' as a 'national evil'.[24] His triumph, in securing the establishment in 1903 of the Economics and Politics Tripos, he saw as a blow against the historicist leanings of the new Faculty of Commerce at Birmingham (headed by Ashley) and the new LSE (headed by Hewins). Marshall's hugely patronizing comment on Hewins in 1897 that he was 'dominantly historical, but can

---

[21] J. Maloney, 'Marshall, Cunningham, and the Emerging Economics Profession', *Econ. Hist. Rev.* 2nd Ser. xxix (1976), pp. 440–51.
[22] Ibid., p. 448.
[23] Ibid., pp. 444–5.
[24] Quoted R. Skidelsky, *John Maynard Keynes*, vol. 1 (1983), p. 45.

reason straight'[25] encapsulates an attitude of mind amply demonstrated, though sometimes even less charitably, by some 'new economic historians' three-quarters of a century or so later. Those averse to quantification and mathematics have variously been labelled as confused, irrational, dogmatic, antiquarian, vulnerable, and resentful, not to say ignorant, much as Marx had described Malthus as a baboon.[26] And it is nicely appropriate that the first editorial act of the 28-year-old Maynard Keynes, on his appointment to the editorship of the *Economic Journal* in 1911, was to turn down a contribution from the 62-year-old Cunningham. It was, he said, 'the most complete wash and had nothing to do with economics'.[27]

Such Cambridge-based joustings were not confined to the Fens in their impact. Many of the rebels and outsiders went to teach elsewhere. Ashley taught at Toronto and Harvard and then went to Birmingham as the Professor of Commerce in the new faculty of that name. Hewins went from Oxford to teach in the University Extension movement in the north of England, before being recruited to the LSE by the Webbs (whose own early writings were valuable contributions to a sort of economic history though their prime interest was *not* in economic matters at all but in government). Meredith left Cambridge for LSE and Manchester; Unwin left Oxford for study in Germany before going to Edinburgh and then Manchester. Cambridge had no chair in economic history until 1928 nor Oxford until 1931. Not every economic historian was a rebel. Thorold Rogers taught orthodox economics at Oxford, was a member of Parliament, and a close friend of Cobden. He observed in 1891 that many years earlier he had begun 'to suspect that much of the political economy which was currently in authority was a collection of logomachies,

---

[25] Quoted Maloney, p. 445.

[26] For some examples of this labelling (mainly in the USA) see P. D. McClelland, *Causal Explanation and Model Building in History, Economics and the New Economic History* (New York, 1975), pp. 147, 192, 214, 220, 243. The animal analogy from Marx is quoted in Keith Thomas, *Man and the Natural World* (1983), p. 47.

[27] Quoted Skidelsky, *Keynes*, I, p. 207.

which had but little relation to the facts of social life'.[28]
Nevertheless, he set out thereafter to discover more about the
historical facts of working men's lives, not to develop or
embrace a different sort of economics. In practice he founded
no school and, save in his factual work on prices and wages,
left a lesser mark on the subject than Cunningham or Ashley.
George Unwin, though he studied with Schmoller in Berlin
and though his *Industrial Organization in the Sixteenth and Seventeenth Centuries* bears the imprint of Germanic methods, reacted
in time against the obsession with the function of the state so
characteristic of the German school. He did not, however,
rebel against theoretical economics; at heart he was a sensitive
liberal in the Manchester tradition. He made a deeply sympathetic impact on both R. H. Tawney and T. S. Ashton.[29]
But he belongs, so to speak, to the second generation of
pioneers; peace with Marshall was in the process of
negotiation.

III

It was, then, within old faculties of History, or such new ones
as Commerce, that were provided the university niches in
which the new specialists taught. So, in old age, Trevelyan
could recall that Harrow, where he had been taught history by
Townsend Warner, supplied a particular preparation for 'the
Cambridge History School, then based on Stubbs and on
Economic History'. The latter, he added, was a new field; but
as for the former, 'I had already broken the back of Stubbs at
school'.[30] The fact that economic history could be thus accommodated within, or at any rate alongside, orthodox British
historiography testified to some changes in that discipline,
parallel to those affecting political economy. Like the latter, it

[28] J. E. Thorold Rogers, *The Economic Interpretation of History* (1891), p. vi.
[29] R. H. Tawney (ed.), *Studies in Economic History: the Collected Papers of George Unwin*
(1927), p. xxxvii. On Unwin's influence on Ashton, see below, pp. 84–5.
[30] Trevelyan, *Autobiography*, pp. 11–12.

shed some of its extreme insularity; and it also lost some of its preoccupation with ancient freedoms and the constitution. Just as one remarkable professor of law, Henry Maine, left his mark on social and economic thinking so, rather later, did another, Frederick Maitland, working in a very different way, leave a profound impression on the English approach to medieval history. If, at the end of the century, medievalists were thus looking more closely at the interaction of law, custom, and society in the past, so were modernists being made to take greater cognizance of Europe as a whole. One of the main instruments of that change, Lord Acton, had the advantage of combining immense erudition with personal acquaintanceship with many of the leading German historians of the time; and, however ambivalent may have been his views on one of the most famous of them, Leopold von Ranke, his cosmopolitan outlook left its mark upon the pursuit of modern history in Britain.[31]

The native historiographical tendencies of the period seemed to be pointing in diverse directions. J. A. Froude, as an historian of the Tudors and of England's early expansion overseas, stood outside the Whig tradition. His writings exhibited that kind of moral authoritarianism associated with romantic social protest of which Thomas Carlyle was the most notable nineteenth-century exemplar. Like Carlyle, whose biography he wrote, Froude disapproved strongly of the *laissez-faire* tenets of political economy; and some amount of social history of a descriptive kind surfaced from time to time in his work. Nevertheless, a passage from a lecture which he gave in 1864 nicely epitomizes a prevalent view of history, which had no doubts about the lowly position of matters economic and material.

And it is precisely in this debatable ground of low motives and noble emotions—in the struggle, ever failing, yet ever renewed, to carry

---

[31] On Acton and Ranke, see H. Butterfield, *Man on his Past* (Cambridge, 1955), pp. 86–95.

truth and justice into the administration of human society; in the establishment of states and in the overthrow of tyrannies; in the rise and fall of creeds; in the world of ideas; in the character and deeds of the great actors in the drama of life; where good and evil fight out their everlasting battle, now ranged in opposite camps, now and more often in the heart, both of them, of each living man—that the true human interest of history resides. The progress of industries, the growth of material and mechanical civilization, are interesting, but they are not the most interesting. They have their reward in the increase of material comforts; but, unless we are mistaken about our nature, they do not highly concern us after all.[32]

A far more evident and genuine interest in the social past appeared in the writings of J. R. Green, whose greatly popular *Short History of the English People* (1874) set out deliberately to distance itself from what, in a famous and much-quoted phrase, he described as 'drum and trumpet' history. Although more 'Whiggish' in sentiment, with its concern for the spirit of individual liberty, Green's work exhibited an interest in a generically, if vaguely, described entity, 'the people of England'. It was an important step in the easing, widening, and popularizing of the Whig interpretation, *en route* for Trevelyan's *Social History of England* some seventy years later. Much further from orthodoxy, and in a very different direction, lay H. T. Buckle. His *History of Civilization in England* asserted a positivistic faith in statistical regularity and physical determinism, though in reality much of the content of the work seems to owe rather less to such a faith than its author supposed. His attempt to construct a composite sort of history failed. He attracted the odium of the orthodox. And he did little, even indirectly, to advance the cause of economic history, despite his confident assertion that the *Wealth of Nations*, 'looking at its ultimate results, is probably the most important book that has ever been written'.[33]

[32] J. A. Froude, *Short Studies on Great Subjects* (ed. D. Ogg, 1963), p. 37. On Froude and social aspects of history, see Burrow, *Liberal Descent*, chap. 9.
[33] H. T. Buckle, *History of Civilization in England* (new edn., 2 vols., 1871), vol. I, p. 214.

From the heterodox and despised Buckle to the brilliant and respected Maitland: the range and intellectual content of British historiography was changing and expanding. As it became professionalized in the universities, it was able to accommodate a handful of pioneer economic historians, mainly wayward protesters against the pretensions of political economy. But accommodation is not absorption. The central concern, the real heart of history, remained the state, be it in its political or constitutional acts or its dynastic or religious forms. As the prefatory note to the first issue of the *English Historical Review* put it, in 1886, history was to be regarded as 'the record of human action, and of thought only in its direct influence upon action. States and politics will therefore [*sic!*] be the chief part of its subject'.[34] Those who saw themselves as the true custodians of historical scholarship eschewed—indeed, barely thought of—any intellectual integration with the economic past. The great opening of national archives imparted momentum to the scholarly editing of source material and reinforced the vision of truth via documentary accuracy. It did little, however, to illuminate the working of past economies. William Stubbs, as Regius Professor of Modern History at Oxford (1866–84), was no more concerned with the possible relationship between government and economy in medieval England than was S. R. Gardiner, as Professor of Modern History at King's College, London (1876–85), in his history of early Stuart England. The celebrated observation by Stubbs' successor at Oxford, E. A. Freeman, that 'history is past politics and politics present history' was echoed by his counterpart (from 1869 to 1895) at Cambridge, J. R. Seeley.[35] Although he possessed a different conception of the nature of historical understanding and did much to enlarge and enliven the teaching of history at Cambridge, Seeley saw the study of the past as essentially a foundation for the study of politics: the University was to be 'a

---

[34] *English Historical Review* I (1886), p. 3.
[35] G. Kitson Clark, 'History at Cambridge', *Historical Journal* XVI (1973), p. 540.

great seminary of politicians'.[36] His successor, Acton, on the other hand, assured his audience at his inaugural lecture in 1895 that 'the first of human concerns is religion and it is the salient feature of modern centuries'.[37] Just as Stubbs (who was, after all, an Anglican bishop) held that the study of history was a form of religious training and that medieval and modern history were co-extensive with ecclesiastical history, so Acton (as a Roman Catholic) saw the need to 'allow some priority to ecclesiastical over civil ... by reason of the graver issues concerned' and its primacy in attracting 'close reasoners and scholars of the higher rank'.[38] He had a lofty vision of history: it was 'the office of historical science to maintain morality as the sole impartial criterion of men and things'.[39] It would hardly be fair to try to assess the thirteen volumes of the *Cambridge Modern History*, which he planned but did not live to see, as an embodiment of that vision; and still less so to ask if it enshrined his even more gnomic contention that 'the higher history is the record of the abiding'.[40] But that great work does provide some illuminating indications of what was seen, by those who carried his plans to fruition, as the nature and concern of modern history and, specifically, the role therein of its economic and social components.

The inclusion of a number of economic history chapters pays tribute to Cunningham's success in fostering the subject in Cambridge, to his having, as Trevelyan later put it, 'conceived and carried out a new idea of the place that economic history should occupy in academic studies'.[41] Cunningham himself contributed a chapter, 'Economic Change', to the first volume (1902). The inclusion, however, in volumes IX (1907) and X (1909) of chapters by a young Cambridge historian,

---

[36] Quoted Sheldon Rothblatt, *The Revolution of the Dons: Cambridge and Society in Victorian England* (Cambridge, 1968), p. 169; also chap. 5 *passim*.

[37] Lord Acton, *Lectures on Modern History* (1907), p. 8.

[38] Ibid., pp. 3, 12, 328, n. 44.

[39] Quoted Butterfield, *Man on his Past*, p. 96.

[40] Quoted ibid., p. 97.

[41] Trevelyan, *Autobiography*, p. 22.

J. H. Clapham, was a product of Marshall's sponsorship. For, in November 1897, when Acton was planning the *History*, he invited Marshall to provide a contribution on the economic history of England. Marshall declined but set out views which clearly pointed to a possible contributor:

I feel that the absence of any tolerable account of the economic development of England during the last century and a half is a disgrace to the land, and a grievous hindrance to the right understanding of the economic problems of our time. London and Cambridge are the only places where the work is likely to be done well; but till recently the man for the work had not appeared. But now I think the man is in sight. Clapham has more analytic faculty than any thorough historian whom I have ever taught; his future work is I think still uncertain; a little force would I think turn him this way or that. If you could turn him towards XVIII and XIX century economic history economists would ever be grateful to you . . . [42]

No doubt the sentiments expressed also contained an implied tilt at Cunningham and the historical economists. Nevertheless, when volume XI appeared, it had not only a chapter by Clapham, 'Great Britain and Free Trade, 1841–52' but also one by J. S. Nicholson on 'The British Economists'. The final textual volume, XII (1910), even went so far as to include a chapter on 'Social Movements' by Sidney Webb.

These chapters represented a real measure of recognition in an aspect of historiography only relatively recently brought into the sight of British historians. But, of course, they remained entirely isolated contributions. The *Cambridge Modern*, as a whole, was overwhelmingly directed towards the conventional topics within national frontiers. Such an arrangement followed more or less inevitably from the announcement by its General Editors in their Introduction that 'the two main features of modern history are the development of nationalities and the growth of individual freedom'.[43]

[42] Marshall to Acton, 13 November 1897, quoted in H. Butterfield, 'Sir John Clapham, 1873–1946', *Cambridge Historical Journal* VIII (1946), pp. 115–16. See also Collini, Winch, and Burrow, *Noble Science of Politics*, pp. 326–7.

[43] *Cambridge Modern History* vol. I (Cambridge, 1902), p. 3.

They uttered not a sound about the transformation of the economic world of 'The Renaissance' (the title of volume I) into the economic world of 'The Latest Age' (treated in volume XII). And nowhere in any of the volumes is there any significant attempt to integrate the economic with the political, the social with the intellectual. So far as that was concerned, Millar and Smith might never have published a word. Such notions, like those about the development of a national economy, were regarded and continued to be regarded by orthodox historians as unprofessional and unscholarly.[44]

IV

This penetration, albeit limited, of academic curricula by economic history was not a product solely of intellectual ferment amongst historians and economists within the universities. A variety of publications and activities had signalled growing and very diverse interests in the economic and social past, both recent and remote.

Some of the publications had testified to enthusiasm for economic liberalism, free trade, and the achievements of what came to be called the industrial revolution. Statistical compilations, such as McCulloch's *Dictionary*, were, as already noted, variations of the eighteenth-century position represented by Anderson and Macpherson. This line was continued in, for example, G. R. Porter's *Progress of the Nation*, which first appeared in 1836 and had gone through a number of editions by 1910. Thomas Tooke—merchant, financier, enthusiastic free trader, and organizer of the celebrated London merchants' petition of 1821—had collaborated with William Newmarch in producing their *History of Prices 1793–1856*, which appeared in six volumes between 1838 and 1857. Tooke was also indirectly responsible for the stimulation of economic

[44] See H. Butterfield, 'Some Trends in Scholarship, 1868–1968, in the Field of Modern History', *Transactions of the Royal Historical Society* 5th Ser. XIX (1969), pp. 174–6.

history in a different way. In 1859, shortly after his death, a group of his friends endowed, at King's College, London, the Tooke Professorship of Economic Science and Statistics. This was a part-time chair and amongst those who occupied it during the nineteenth century were Thorold Rogers, Cunningham, and Hewins.[45] King's College, London, also had another keen advocate of free trade occupying a chair outside the conventional academic discipline in the person of Leone Levi, Professor of Commerce and Commercial Law. His *History of British Commerce and of the Economic Progress of the British Nation, 1763–1870*, which appeared in 1872, belongs to the same genre as Porter's work.

A slightly different variant, though again with a clear eighteenth-century ancestry, was the vogue for technical and scientific dictionaries. Such early nineteenth-century examples as Abraham Rees's *Cyclopaedia of Arts, Sciences and Literature* (1819) were followed by those with a much more evident admixture of praise for popular political economy and factory production, the most notable example being Andrew Ure's *Dictionary of Arts, Manufactures and Mines*. It first came out in 1839, only four years after his explicit panegyric on the factory, *The Philosophy of Manufactures* (1835), and had run to seven editions and four volumes by 1878–9. Histories of industries, normally those which experienced great expansion during this period, represented a type of historical enterprise wholly outside the world of Freeman and Stubbs. Such works also often embodied eulogies of free trade. Edward Baines' *History of the Cotton Manufacture in Great Britain* (1835) and J. James, *History of Worsted Manufacture* (1857) are merely two of many examples. Yet another, and more obviously popular, form was represented by Samuel Smiles' early exercises in business hagiography and the virtues of self-help: *The Life of George Stephenson* (1857) and *The Lives of the Engineers* (which appeared in three volumes in 1861–2).

Such writings are merely instances on the edges of a new

[45] In 1920 the Tooke Professorship went to LSE and became a full-time chair.

sort of historical curiosity in Victorian Britain. It was a
curiosity in which was mingled some pride, often locally
generated, in the nation's economic and technical achievements and some diffused and romantic notions about the
nation's past. Its most evident and most bulky manifestation
was the disguising of that very new thing, the railway station,
as that very old thing, the medieval Gothic cathedral. St
Pancras is the most obvious example. And not only railway
stations. Town halls in the new industrial towns, offices or
warehouses in London, and the new mansions of the newly
rich, fitted with the latest in plumbing but garnished with
medieval statuary: all were made to testify at once to continuity and to change. Nor was it just a matter of architectural
style. Local societies devoted to antiquarian, topographical,
and archaeological interests—descendants of the county historians and antiquaries of the eighteenth century—began to
concern themselves with the preservation of ancient buildings
just as the new works of industrialism sprouted around
them.[46]

But all was not acceptance of the new order. Perhaps the
most potent immediate force helping to stimulate the later
nineteenth-century concern for the economic past was unease.
It had more than one origin: middle-class social guilt at
poverty amidst wealth; distaste for aggressive industrialism;
nostalgia for a supposed age of pre-industrial bliss; and, especially pervasive, apprehension at evident set-backs in Britain's
economic performance.

In 1885—a mere thirty-four years after the Great Exhibition had seemed to register the triumph of *laissez-faire*, of
orthodox political economy, and of all those wisdoms trum-
peted in their totally different styles by McCulloch and
Macaulay—a Royal Commission was appointed to enquire
into the current depression in industry and trade. Ten years

---

[46] On these developments see C. Dellheim, *The Face of the Past: the Preservation of the Medieval Inheritance in Victorian England* (Cambridge, 1982) and M. Girouard, *The Victorian Country House* (1979).

later, another was doing the same for agriculture. Whether a so-called 'Great Depression' existed at that time has been debated by a much later generation of economic historians. For contemporaries, however, a real sense of current depression was induced by two decades of fluctuating and generally falling profits and prices from the mid-1870s to the mid-1890s, along with an awareness of stiffening competition at home and overseas, as well as of being overtaken by Germany and the USA in certain key areas of production. It was just such a context that helped to undermine faith in orthodox political economy. Whatever the inadequacies of the historical economics of the alternative school or, conversely, the gains registered by the marginal revolution and the Marshallian economics which emerged, there was, meanwhile, a good deal of justification for Ashley's comments in his Toronto inaugural of 1888.

Ten or fifteen years ago Political Economy occupied, in English-speaking countries, no very dignified or useful position ... Few clever men really believed in it as a useful possession in after-life. Nobody was inclined to deny that it was all true—'so far as it went'—but there was a sort of feeling that it didn't go very far ...

Meanwhile the very term Political Economy stank in the nostrils of intelligent working men. Mechanics Institutes had been fed upon it for half a century to show artizans how that everything in the industrial world was for the best ... [47]

So, at this juncture in British history, it is far from surprising that amongst the pioneer economic historians, who were also rebels against orthodox political economy, there should have been some active participants in the tariff-reform movement. Although taking up differing political stances in the 'social-imperialist' line of thought, and, consequently, in their relationship to Joseph Chamberlain's tariff-reform campaign, Cunningham, Ashley, and Hewins were all deeply involved in anti-free-trade activity.[48] Cunningham's 'nationalist'

[47] Quoted in Anne Ashley, *William James Ashley, a Life* (1932), p. 49.
[48] B. Semmel, *Imperialism and Social Reform* (1960).

approach to protectionism is apparent in his sympathetic treatment, as an historian, of the whole complex of thought and policy which Adam Smith had deplored as the mercantile system. Cunningham's commendation of it stands in stark contrast to the derisory jeers with which McCulloch had accompanied his historical treatment of that same era. Ashley's involvement in protectionist and imperialist policy-recommendations effectively dates from his return to England and the Birmingham chair. His historical writings did not provide justification, in terms of sympathy for mercantilism, but he had a more subtle and complex approach to the economic issues than Cunningham. His ideas drew inevitably upon the German school; and, indeed, he was one of the very few British economic historians to show much awareness of Marx, some of whose ideas he accepted and some he rejected. With a good deal of justification, Ashley came to be seen as the chief academic supporter of Chamberlain's tariff-reform policy.[49] Against Hewins' lesser direct significance as an early British economic historian, must be put his indirect importance for the growth of the subject, as the first Director of the LSE. Chosen by the Webbs as the leader of the new Fabian institution, Hewins was a very enthusiastic imperialist and protectionist. So also were his immediate successors in that post—Halford Mackinder and William Pember Reeves. Although neither of these two was an economic historian by academic affiliation, the first three directors of LSE together helped indirectly to further the identification of the new subject with economic heterodoxy. Mackinder, indeed, was appointed by the Webbs to the directorship precisely when Hewins resigned to become secretary to the Tariff Commission set up by the protectionists in 1903 to prepare and publicize their case.[50]

Whatever the strength of their commitment to tariff-reform

---

[49] On Cunningham's and Ashley's contributions to 'social imperialism', see Semmel, op. cit., chaps. 10 and 11.

[50] On Mackinder, see Semmel, chap. 8.

or 'social-imperialism', it was unease at the increasingly evident manifestations of poverty amidst wealth, of slums amidst splendour, that imparted the most powerful moral momentum to the pioneers of economic history in Britain. A mere slackening of the pace of industrial growth was one thing; the revelations of Charles Booth's survey of working-class London or of Seerbohm Rowntree's similar study of York were quite another. The diverse sounds of literary opposition to industrialism, from Southey or Carlyle to Ruskin or William Morris, hardly themselves melded into a strong and unified voice of protest. But the strengthening of trade unions, the implications of a widened electorate, of agrarian depression and urban discontent, of new industries, new unemployment, and new challenges everywhere seemed to pose problems demanding action rather than rhetoric; and stimulated a slumbering sense of middle-class social guilt.

Here, for the advance of economic history in Britain, a key role was played by Arnold Toynbee and his *Lectures on the Industrial Revolution*. Toynbee evidently left a very deep impression on a circle of contemporaries and students. A young man of perilously poor health, he combined intelligence and wide reading with social compassion and religious convictions. In 1878, at the age of twenty-six, he was appointed to a tutorship at Balliol College, Oxford. His main task was to lecture on political economy to candidates for the Indian Civil Service—a nice echo of the earlier tasks of Malthus and Richard Jones at Haileybury. He also gave lectures on 'the industrial revolution' (his own title) to those reading history and found time to pursue sundry external commitments, including giving highly successful lectures to gatherings of working men both in London and in various northern industrial towns. This aggregation of self-imposed work proved too much for his health; by March 1883 he was dead. Only a couple of months earlier, in the course of one of these lectures, he had delivered himself of what was to become a classical statement of bourgeois social contrition.

We—the middle classes, I mean, not merely the very rich—we have neglected you . . . I think we are changing. If you would only believe it and trust us, I think that many of us would spend our lives in your service . . . we have wronged you; we have sinned against you grievously . . . if you will forgive us—nay, whether you will forgive us or not—we will serve you, we will devote our lives to your service.[51]

And so on. Such sentiments were to leave their mark on a generation of social reformers and on the nature of economic and social history as studied in Britain. Meanwhile, in the year after his death, and as a consequence of the strong impact which he made as a lecturer, his book came into being in the form of a posthumous revision by Alfred (later Lord) Milner from the notes by undergraduate listeners, of whom the most important was Ashley. It went through five editions by 1908 and was subsequently reprinted several times; it did not go out of print until 1927 and was then again reprinted as late as 1969.[52]

As an historical study it is clearly unsatisfactory in structure and coverage alike; it does not match the standards of scholarship evident in, say, Ashley's own *Introduction to Economic History and Theory*. But such criteria are inappropriate for judging such a work. The powerful impression which it left arose from three interrelated features, which shine through this *mélange* of extended lecture notes on classical economics, the industrial revolution, working-class standards of life, and the future of industrial democracy. One was a passionate concern for what a later generation was to call the 'democratic decencies'. Much influenced by the philosophical teachings of T. H. Green, Toynbee, in G. N. Clark's words, was 'the young Paladin of liberal social reform, fighting for democracy and against *laissez-faire*, against socialism, against class-war,

[51] Quoted at length in Beatrice Webb, *My Apprenticeship* (1926, edn. 1950), pp. 157–8.
[52] Arnold Toynbee, *Lectures on the Industrial Revolution in England. Popular Addresses, Notes and other Fragments* (1884; repr. with Introduction by T. S. Ashton, Newton Abbott, 1969).

against the creeds but also against irreligion'.[53] This crusading spirit derived strength from a second, more theoretic and rather less obvious quality: an attempt to understand and preserve what was worthwhile in the teachings of orthodox political economists; to modify them but not to replace them by the inductive approach of the historical economists; and to set the ideas in their historical contexts. The analytic exegesis was neither sustained nor thorough but within a brief compass a quality of tolerance and understanding is more evident than in some of the shriller contributions to this debate. The third, and for economic history in Britain, the most potent practical feature was his use of the term 'industrial revolution'. It was certainly not the first use but it was he who, so to speak, put it in capital letters in British history. He presented it as a more or less cataclysmic event, which transformed ideas as well as economic life.

The essence of the Industrial Revolution is the substitution of competition for the medieval regulations which had previously controlled the production and distribution of wealth. On this account it is not only one of the most important facts of English history, but Europe owes to it the growth of two great systems of thought—Economic Science and its antithesis, Socialism.[54]

Before its arrival Adam Smith had displayed his 'complete and unhesitating trust in individual self-interest'. But after Smith:

We now approach a darker period—a period as disastrous and as terrible as any through which a nation ever passed; disastrous and terrible, because, side by side with a great increase of wealth was seen an enormous increase of pauperism; and production on a vast scale, the result of free competition, led to a rapid alienation of classes and to the degradation of a large body of producers.[55]

With such passages as these, Toynbee not only influenced

[53] G. N. Clark, *The Idea of the Industrial Revolution* (Glasgow, 1952), p. 21.
[54] Toynbee, *Lectures*, p. 85.
[55] Ibid., p. 84.

the Webbs and the Hammonds but, indirectly and unconsciously, provided material for the curricula of economic history courses in Britain for generations to come and ensured a preoccupation with a particular topic amounting to almost total obsession. If his surviving monument is Toynbee Hall, his educational monument is a multitude of examination questions on The Industrial Revolution. But the legacy was not merely confined to that particular phenomenon or metaphor. The notion of economic history as a path to social reform was, for a long time, to permeate its study and exposition in Britain, whatever the topic, be it the nineteenth-century cotton industry or sixteenth-century enclosures, eighteenth-century commerce or fourteenth-century peasants. In ensuring this, Toynbee was a figure of lasting influence and importance for the development of economic history in twentieth-century Britain.

Yet, in one significant respect, his influence failed. In his introductory lecture on the industrial revolution he told his audience that he had chosen that period because it was then that modern political economy had begun. Despite Smith and Malthus and largely because of Ricardo, he added, economic science had been too much dissociated from history. So there was an advantage to be had in combining history and political economy—a combination which existed in his time at both Oxford and Cambridge. He went on to make the vital corollary: 'history also is better understood when studied in connection with political economy'.[56] The subsequent teaching in Britain both of economics and of history managed nearly, if not quite totally, to ignore that recommendation.

It is time to start looking at that subsequent teaching.

[56] Toynbee, op. cit., p. 28.

5

Reformists and Neutralists

A very large number of those who are attracted by Economic History are not content to regard it merely as a department of study to be pursued for the sake of obtaining further
knowledge of the past, but look on it as a guide which may
enable us to make further progress in the future.

W. Cunningham, *Hints on the Study of
English Economic History* (1919)[1]

In 1908, two men took decisions (unknown to each other)
which were to leave an enduring mark on the development of
economic history as an intellectual activity in Britain. The 28-
year-old R. H. Tawney, a classics graduate from Balliol
College, Oxford, began to teach the subject to working men in
Rochdale and Longton; and the 35-year-old J. H. (later Sir
John) Clapham returned to King's College, Cambridge, and
began a series of economic history lectures which he continued
to give for many years. The one decision led to a group of
immensely influential works on the economic and social history of Tudor and Stuart England; the other to magisterial
volumes on the economic history of Victorian and Edwardian
Britain. Tawney's name symbolizes the approach to the subject which did much to identify it with the cause of social
reform and, to some extent, socialism; that of Clapham stands
for quantification, some limited use of the tools of neo-classical
economics, and an attempted stance of ethical neutralism in
relation to the course of economic change. The names are
symbolic, the achievements reality. Each came to be part of

---

[1] A pamphlet in a series called 'Helps for Students of History' published by the
Society for Promoting Christian Knowledge.

two wider and more diverse groupings of economic historians, as the subject became established in academic curricula.

For the purposes of identification, I have given to the two groupings the labels 'reformists' and 'neutralists' The former[2] is simply a convenient label for those whose writings on the economic and social past carry messages, direct or indirect and in varying codes, in favour of a reform of the present. The label 'neutralist' signifies a diverse grouping whose common feature is that they do not carry such messages. This latter label has to include the extremes of those who seek to avoid, by one method or another, the making of any moral judgement about the past and those who, usually in response to messages by the reformists about the past, find themselves in a posture of defence, thereby evidently losing their neutrality. It is not to be taken as an exactly literal definition but it should serve to identify a broadly recognizable grouping. The categories may obviously include, but are not co-terminus with, those respectively labelled 'pessimists' and 'optimists' in the controversy about the standard of living during the industrial revolution in the UK.[3]

Not all economic hstorians fall neatly into the two categories suggested by the labels. Nevertheless, this dichotomy, and the hopes and controversies aroused thereby, was to remain broadly characteristic of the pursuit of economic history in Britain for many years to come and is by no means defunct today.

I

The main common characteristic of the reformist position was some degree of aversion to industrial capitalism. The range was wide. It encompassed such variants as the Christian

[2] I have borrowed the term, with permission, from Dr Peter Clarke's most valuable study, *Liberals and Social Democrats* (Cambridge, 1978) though it does not here have the same precision as he gave it to denote a particular attitude to political and social reform.

[3] See below, pp. 80, 84.

socialism of Tawney, seeking to re-spiritualize industrial man; the passionate liberalism of the Hammonds, confronting the historical spectacle of enclosing landlords of the eighteenth century; the radical socialism of Cole and Postgate, exhibiting the working classes as battered victims of ruthless capitalists of the industrial revolution; or, later, the Marxist vocabulary of Christopher Hill, directed at Tudor and Stuart gentry who were presented as busily beating down the living standards of the English poor. It may clearly be categorized as an inverted and economic version of the Whig interpretation of history. Just as the Macaulay–Trevelyan sort of history produced 'a story which is the ratification if not the glorification of the present',[4] so the reformist group of economic historians produced a story which represented the disapprobation, if not the vilification, of the capitalist present.

This is not in the least to impute intellectual dishonesty or to suggest that a particular vision of the economic past was being projected simply to serve immediate political ends. On the contrary, much, though certainly not all, of the work of the reformists has been of a high scholarly standard. Nor is it to imply that, amongst economic historians, the reformists alone have been addicted to Whig history. Perhaps more than most sorts of history, the economic sort tends towards studying the past with reference to the present. Why otherwise study the past? The retort is obvious and has been made by neutralists as well as by reformists. Economics-minded neutralists have also taken this line, though often with different intent. What distinguishes the Whig history of the reformists is the grafting of a sense of middle-class social guilt onto a class-based analysis of the past. Thereby was generated moral disapproval of a particular social class—frequently the historian's own class—seen as operating an historical process which culminated in the present economic and social order. Moreover,

---

[4] H. Butterfield, *The Whig Interpretation of History* (1931; Pelican edn., Harmondsworth, 1973), p. 9.

that disapproval was generated not merely by the inherent nature of the actions but by the position and supposed function of the class performing the actions. In its most extreme form, this produces a picture of the economic past peopled by 'goodies' and 'baddies', by heroes and villains performing in a still-running drama.

The link with Karl Marx seems obvious but it is not, at least in the earlier works of the reformists. Middle-class social guilt was of much greater consequence. It was a powerful weapon in its appeal to many of the more socially sensitive members of a class, brought up in the Christian tradition, which had long exhibited ambiguous attitudes towards the making of profits. It was carried, in one form or another, by virtually all of those in the reformist category. As already indicated in Chapter 4, amongst the pioneers of economic history Arnold Toynbee was probably the most influential standard-bearer in this middle-class crusade. In 1926 Beatrice Webb—herself in her ardent days as social investigator, Beatrice Potter, the very embodiment of it—called it a 'consciousness of sin amongst men of intellect and men of property'. She provided a list of its variegated forms and their historical progenitors:

... at first philanthropic and practical—Oastler, Shaftesbury and Chadwick; then literary and artistic—Dickens, Carlyle, Ruskin and William Morris, and finally, analytic, historical and explanatory —in his latter days, John Stuart Mill; Karl Marx and his English interpreters; Alfred Russel Wallace and Henry George; Arnold Toynbee and the Fabians. I might perhaps add a theological category—Charles Kingsley, F. D. Maurice, General Booth and Cardinal Manning.[5]

There are some odd bedfellows here; and not everyone might today be convinced that Marx and Manning had identical senses of sin. It serves, however, to point to some recognizable roots of the reformist historians. Beatrice Webb's

[5] Webb, *My Apprenticeship* (1926; edn. 1950), pp. 154–5.

quotation from Canon Barnett—founder of Toynbee Hall, another quintessential monument to that sense—precisely identifies a relevant sentiment: 'the sense of sin has been the starting point of progress'.[6] And she also quoted with notable approval, and at length, those previously cited expressions of social penitence uttered in 1883 by Arnold Toynbee,[7] 'one of the noblest and most original of these latter-day confessors'.[8]

Although this attitude of mind on the part of the reformists has necessarily made their sort of history class-based, it did not, at least initially, have the systematic class-based analytical structure inherent in Marxism. Marx's ideas were certainly not ignored by such pioneers as Ashley, Cunningham, and Unwin, but what appeal they had arose, on the one hand, from current disillusionment with orthodox political economy and, on the other, from reaction against orthodox British historiography and its narrow obsession with political and constitutional history. Thorold Rogers, friend of Cobden and of conventional political economy, could write *The Economic Interpretation of History* without any reference whatever to Marx. Unwin commented: 'Marx is truer than Seeley. He did not get his history right, but he was trying to get at the right kind of history. The orthodox historians ignore all the most significant facts in human development'.[9] This was characteristic of the pioneer's attitude: polite disbelief in Marx's version of history but a recognition of the importance of the issues with which he was concerned.[10] Nor did Marx's dogmatic materialism readily appeal to such minds as those of Toynbee and Unwin, the Hammonds, or Tawney. Whatever the impact of Marx on the political ideas of the Liberals, Socialists, and Fabians, during the three decades before World War

[6] Quoted ibid., p. 155.
[7] Above, p. 60.
[8] *My Apprenticeship*, p. 157.
[9] Tawney (ed.), *Studies in Economic History: Collected Papers of George Unwin*, pp. lxvi and 4–5.
[10] See also E. J. Hobsbawm, 'Dr. Marx and his Critics' in his *Labouring Men* (1964), pp. 238–71.

I, it was muted in its influence on the early economic and social historians, even on those who moved in the same intellectual circles.

The soil of the 1930s proved more fruitful for the growth of Marxist historians in Britain. From the age-group which went through adolescence or early manhood during the 1930s came a number who, for sundry well-rehearsed reasons, found compelling not simply the political Left but the Marxist version of history. They made their mark in the decades after World War II.[11] Meanwhile, however, the unquestionably dominant figure amongst the reformists was, of course, Tawney, with the Hammonds as important runners-up. Together, they exerted a powerful influence, not only on the relatively small but growing number of students of economic history before World War II, but on some of those who came in on the flood-tide of post-war enthusiasm.

Tawney's dominance of the economic history scene in Britain rested on far more than his position as a highly respected figure of the intellectual Left. Indeed, from the 1930s onwards, his voice in those quarters became less powerful, as his disenchantment with the Labour party deepened and as such shriller voices as those of John Strachey and Harold Laski made themselves heard. His heyday as a sage of a certain type of Christian socialism was marked by the publication of his two works of social philosophy, *The Acquisitive Society* (1921) and *Equality* (1931). They embodied those of his social and political thoughts which had germinated in the years before and just after World War I. Dr Jay Winter has admirably surveyed and analysed these early ideas and ideals; and Mr Ross Terrill has considered some other and later aspects of Tawney's 'socialism as fellowship'.[12] My concern here is neither with Tawney as social philosopher nor with his specific historical findings but rather with the nature of his

[11] See below, pp. 111–14.
[12] J. M. Winter, 'R. H. Tawney's Early Political Thought', *Past and Present* 47 (1970), pp. 71–96; Ross Terrill, *R. H. Tawney and his Times* (1974).

outstanding appeal as an economic historian and the way in which his contribution to the discipline shaped its growth in Britain.[13] That some of that appeal derived from his political posture is obvious. But as an historian his stature almost certainly gained from his failure as a political activist. Had he been successful when he contested parliamentary seats, he would not, I suspect, have become an expert politician but the study of economic history would surely have been the loser.

It was precisely because Tawney was essentially a moralist, seen as operating above the rough-and-tumble of political wrangling, manœvring, and in-fighting, that his historical works, with their complex inner messages about contemporary situations, could appeal as strongly as they did to both idealistic artisans and middle-class intellectuals plagued with social guilt. For all that it dealt with Tudor England, *The Agrarian Problem of the Sixteenth Century* (1912) was as much an indirect tract for the times as was R. E. Prothero's *English Farming Past and Present*, which appeared in the same year, or J. L. and B. Hammond's *The Village Labourer* of 1911. Prothero's work can as reasonably be considered as an anti-socialist apologia for the existing structure of landownership as both Tawney's and the Hammonds' books can be regarded as radical anti-landlord tracts.[14] In fact, all three were much more than that, surviving as historical enquiries, carrying insights which transcended the political convictions of their authors. Tawney made it clear that he had no love for the landowning gentry and aristocracy. He went further, however, in presenting the agrarian changes of Tudor England as part of a divide, not just in matters of farming and land tenure, but in the nature of the social, economic, and moral world occupied by our forebears.

[13] A more detailed and rather different consideration of him as historian will be found in the Introduction, 'Tawney the historian', in J. M. Winter (ed.), *History and Society. Essays by R. H. Tawney* (1978), pp. 1–43.

[14] See O. R. McGregor's Introduction to Lord Ernle (R. E. Prothero), *English Farming Past and Present* (1912; 6th edn., 1961).

In truth the agrarian revolution is but a current in the wake of mightier movements. The new world, which is painfully rising in so many English villages, is a tiny mirror of the new world which, on a mightier stage, is ushering modern history in amid storms and convulsions. The spirit which revolts against authority, frames a science that will subdue nature to its service, and thrusts the walls of the universe asunder into space, is the same—we must not hesitate to say it—as that which on the lips of grasping landlords and stubborn peasants wrangles over the respected merits of 'several' and 'common', weighs the profits of pasture in an economic scale against the profits of arable, batters down immemorial customs, and, regarding neither the honour of God nor the welfare of this realm of England, brings the livings of many into the hands of one.[15]

This seductive mixture of Christian ethics and economic generalities demonstrated its potency in what was to become the best-known and most widely read of Tawney's books, *Religion and the Rise of Capitalism*. Based on the Holland Memorial Lectures given in 1922 and published as a book in 1926, it was reprinted many times both before and after World War II, was translated into several languages, and achieved sales figures which put it into the best-seller class. But not because people were yearning to read about Max Weber's ideas on Calvin and the Protestant Ethic or even on Puritanism and English economic life in the seventeenth century. Rather, it appealed because it contained messages for bewildered searchers after enlightenment in a world which had lost many of its spiritual and intellectual signposts after a long and terrible war. As was remarked by W. H. B. Court—later Professor of Economic History at Birmingham University but a student in the 1920s—it was 'one of the books which everyone read'.[16] It was one thing to read that:

---

[15] *The Agrarian Problem of the Sixteenth Century* (1912; paperback edn., New York, 1967), pp. 408–9.

[16] W. H. B. Court, *Scarcity and Choice in History* (1970), p. 18. Court's autobiographical essay, 'Growing up in an Age of Anxiety' and his memoirs of Tawney and Clapham, all of which appear in this book, shed much light on the appeal of economic history to a sensitive student and scholar in the inter-war years.

Puritanism was the schoolmaster of the English middle classes. It heightened their values, sanctified without eradicating their convenient vices, and gave them an inexpugnable assurance that, behind virtues and vices alike, stood the majestic and inexorable laws of an omnipotent Providence, without whose foreknowledge not a hammer could beat upon the forge, nor figure be added to the ledger.[17]

It was rather more to add:

Compromise is as impossible between the Church of Christ and the idolatry of wealth, which is the practical religion of capitalist societies, as it was between the Church and the State idolatry of the Roman Empire.[18]

The messages gained greatly in their intensity from the manner in which they were written. Tawney as stylist occupied a class similar to that of Macaulay, even though the manner and the matter were very different. His style could, a little unkindly, be called modified Mandarin toughened with irony. Certainly it sometimes has some of the qualities enumerated by Cyril Connolly in his definition of the Mandarin style: '. . . characterized by long sentences with many dependent clauses, by the use of the subjunctive and conditional, . . . allusions, metaphors, long images . . . '. And there are times when it undoubtedly makes 'the written word as unlike as possible to the spoken one'.[19] It was, however, redeemed by a strength and vigour drawn from the English of the Authorized Version, by a highly effective use of irony, and by the fortunately frequent recourse to the clarity demanded by a particular historical subject-matter. It is likely, too, that potential flights into the Mandarin manner were often grounded by the habits of style, more prosaic but still sinewy and compelling, which he used in the substantial amount of

[17] R. H. Tawney, *Religion and the Rise of Capitalism* (1936 edn.), pp. 211–12.
[18] Ibid., p. 286.
[19] Cyril Connolly, *Enemies of Promise* (1938; paperback edn., Harmondsworth, 1961), pp. 25, 29–30.

journalism written for the *Manchester Guardian* over many years.

Some of Tawney's impact arose not merely from the persuasiveness of what he wrote, but from the simple fact that he wrote a great deal. He was a very long way indeed from one of those neurotic perfectionists amongst historians who, after one brilliant article, spend the rest of their working lives looking for the evidence to support the ideas which they are never sure are quite worth publishing. Those, in short, who in Tawney's own words 'make a darkness and call it research'.[20] His output of books and learned articles would put many a modern economic historian to shame. The three-volume *Tudor Economic Documents* (1929), edited jointly with Eileen Power, provided the invaluable source material for an almost wholly new topic of historical study. His 'Rise of the Gentry, 1558–1640' and associated articles gave rise to one of the major debates in post-war historiography and supplied a mass of Ph.D. fodder in the battle over 'Tawney's Century'. Nor was it all concerned solely with the sixteenth and seventeenth centuries. He wrote on wages in the chain-making industry in the early twentieth century, on the abolition of economic controls after World War I, on the American labour movement, and his book *Land and Labour in China* (1932) is, in some respects, his most impressive analysis of an economic and social conjunction. All this and more was wholly apart from his sundry activities, sometimes anonymous, as publicist on education, society, politics, and Christianity.[21]

To all of this he added the inestimable advantage—at least for those who knew him or knew of him—of being a very English sort of eccentric. The English are said to adore eccentrics, provided of course that they are likeable and preferably of an acceptable social class. Tawney was all of these things.

---

[20] The words are in his inaugural lecture, 'The Study of Economic History', reprinted in Harte (ed.), *Study*, p. 105.

[21] For references to all these works, see J. M. Winter, *A Bibliography of the Published Writings of R. H. Tawney* (Economic History Society, 1974).

Although he spoke with the accents of Rugby and Balliol, his clothes were bizarrely shabby, his flat in Mecklenberg Square a marvel of disorder, his cottage in the country a rural slum, his professorial absent-mindedness (at least in later years) a model of its kind, his witticisms worth waiting for, and even his wife offered her own eccentricities of hats, cooking, and conversation. But it was real and not a pose. His humanity, integrity, and moral sincerity were as genuine as was his failure to change the mind and soul of capitalist man.

Like other graduates of his class and persuasion, Tawney had started the process of assuaging his own share of social guilt by doing his stint at Toynbee Hall. Barbara Bradby, on the other hand, was practically brought up in it.[22] Her father, a parson and former headmaster of Haileybury, had moved with his family into east London to help Canon Barnett with his work at Toynbee Hall. In 1901, with a First in Greats behind her, she married another parson's offspring, the rising young Liberal journalist, J. L. Hammond. Thereby was created the basis for a literary partnership second only to Tawney in creating the reformist category of social and economic historians in Britain. Unlike Tawney—successively Reader and, in 1931, Professor of Economic History at LSE—the Hammonds took virtually no part in the teaching of the subject nor in the launching of the relevant learned societies and journals. Lawrence Hammond spent his entire working life, save for a brief spell as a Civil Servant from 1907 to 1915, as a journalist, mainly with the *Manchester Guardian*. His wife was chief researcher and co-author of their books.[23]

Their works had a much more limited range than Tawney's; they had a less profound but possibly even wider impact in Britain. Jointly motivated by an all-consuming devotion to Liberal causes, the Hammonds produced from

[22] Clarke, *Liberals and Social Democrats*, p. 80. The paragraphs which follow owe much to Dr Clarke's work. For the Hammonds and the social guilt theme, see p. 158.
[23] Ibid., pp. 80, 154, 158. He did some university extension lecturing in his early years.

1911 onwards a series of books which demonstrated the power of a particular sort of historiography—scholarly but readable and written with burning conviction—to influence the minds of more than one generation. Their trilogy—*The Village Labourer* (1911), *The Town Labourer* (1917), and, the least successful, *The Skilled Labourer* (1919)—presented rural and urban labourers alike as a class trampled down into demoralized poverty, shame, and misery by unthinking landlords and rapacious industrialists in the course of the creation between 1760 and 1830 of what they saw as the 'new civilization' of the Industrial Revolution (with the capital letters taken over from Toynbee).[24] The first two of these books enjoyed a remarkable success, being reprinted many times, and not least when they appeared in paperback in 1948 and 1949. The Hammonds synthesized and extended their findings into general textbook form in *The Rise of Modern Industry* (1925),[25] which again met with considerable success, and in *The Age of the Chartists* (1930), which later reappeared in an amended paperback form as *The Bleak Age* (1947). It was in many ways a remarkable achievement, the *Labourer* trilogy, in particular, being wholly original in its source material, and, from an historiographical viewpoint, in its subject-matter.

Only in a very limited sense, however, could the Hammonds be regarded as having written economic history. It was not simply that Barbara Hammond admitted that she wrote as 'one whose ignorance of mathematics is profound',[26] but that both of them seemed to have remained wholly innocent of any sort of economic theory, explicit or implicit. Economic questions—be they about the nature of demand, the costs of production, or the role of investment—were entirely absent from their reasoning. In this, they provided an

[24] *Town Labourer*, Preface to the first edition.
[25] See the Introduction by R. M. Hartwell to the 9th edn. (1966) for figures of total printing of both this and the *Labourer* trilogy. Also Clarke, *Liberals and Social Democrats*, pp. 155–62, 187–90, 243–52 for much illuminating discussion of the Hammonds and their work.
[26] Quoted Clarke, p. 245.

extreme instance of a general feature of the reformists: ignorance, distaste, or rejection of economics. Tawney knew Marshall's work but in 1913 referred to it in scathing terms:

There is no such thing as a science of economics, nor ever will be. It is just cant, and Marshall's talk as to the need for social problems to be studied by 'the same order of mind which tests the stability of a battleship in bad weather' is twaddle.[27]

Even in later years his view of the subject was suitably summarized by his comment that economics was 'a body of occasionally useful truisms'.[28] At LSE he opposed a proposal to make statistics a compulsory subject,[29] and he came to view its journal *Economica* with increasing dislike as its content of economic history fell and that of theoretical economics rose. A number of later writers in the reformist tradition have similarly eschewed both economics and the quantitative analysis of their subject-matter.[30] So the Hammonds could boldly affirm that 'the Industrial Revolution must be seen . . . as a departure in which man passed definitely from one world to another'[31] yet at the same time pay virtually no heed to the possible economic causes of so allegedly cataclysmic a happening.

The socio-political history which they did write was not simply anti-drum-and-trumpet social history in the manner of J. R. Green. Like Tawney's writings, their books were social tracts for the times. If *The Village Labourer* was thus complementary to *The Agrarian Problem* it was also, on a wholly different level of feeling and experience, an historical counterpart

---

[27] J. M. Winter and D. M. Joslin (eds.), *R. H. Tawney's Commonplace Book* (Cambridge, 1972), p. 72.

[28] Quoted Terrill, *R. H. Tawney*, p. 66. The idea, thought by Ved Mehta to be held by 'many professional historians' that Tawney 'by brilliantly employing economic analysis' had helped to revolutionize the study of history is merely absurd—Ved Mehta, *Fly and Fly Bottle: Encounters with British Intellectuals* (1963), p. 110.

[29] Terrill, *R. H. Tawney*, p. 66.

[30]. See below, pp. 111–12.

[31] *Rise of Modern Industry* (1966 edn.), p. 240.

to George Sturt's *Change in the Village* (1912). The urgent reality of contemporary issues, along with the tilt of the Hammonds' historiography towards the political rather than the economic, is evident in a comment made by Barbara Hammond in September 1910. She observed that in her research, 'the Whig Govt. of 1830 & the present Govt. are quite mixed up in my sentiments & I expect that a good deal of the disgust I feel for the latter is due to the behaviour of the former'.[32] *The Town Labourer* has but one relatively short chapter on economic conditions. Its real thrust is against power and its use or misuse: the war on trade unions, the defences of the poor, the spirit of religion, the mind and the conscience of the rich. *The Rise of Modern Industry* offers a view of the possessors of power which certainly has the appeal of simplicity:

The upper classes divided the world into capital and labour, and they held that the struggle was between custom and initiative, between the prejudices of the poor which hampered industry, and the spirit of acquisition and adventure in the rich which encouraged it.[33]

In their concentration on the industrial revolution, the Hammonds, rather than Tawney, were the direct historiographical heirs of Toynbee. They found the ultimate cause of the social evils of their own day in what they saw as the unrestrained capitalism of that particular age and that particular traumatic event. Tawney viewed the search for profits by seventeenth-century businessmen with distaste, just as he did the similar activities of his own banking and brewing ancestors in eighteenth-century Oxfordshire. Indeed, although he wrote much about the former, nothing would induce him to digress upon the latter. The Hammonds ascribed virtually everything they disliked about the industrial revolution in England to the similar search for profits:

[32] Quoted Clarke, *Liberals and Social Democrats*, p. 156.
[33] *Rise of Modern Industry*, p. 108.

76

This England asked for profits and received profits. Everything turned to profit. The towns had their profitable dirt, their profitable smoke, their profitable slums, their profitable disorder, their profitable ignorance, their profitable despair. The curse of Midas was on this society . . . the new factories and the new furnaces were like the Pyramids, telling of man's enslavement, rather than of his power.[34]

The first generation of economic historians, both the pioneers and the textbook writers, had presented the industrial revolution as sudden, cataclysmic, and productive of suffering for the working class. Although the degree of reaction against classical political economy varied amongst these writers, the picture of that suffering as being peculiarly a product of the theory and rapid practice of economic *laissez-faire* was already on its way to becoming established orthodoxy. The Hammonds, by the very passion and sincerity of their writing, did much to ensure the continuance of the idea of the industrial revolution as, to quote Dr Cannadine, 'nasty, mean, brutish and fast'.[35] They also ensured the continuance of a debate on the social consequences of the industrial revolution well into recent times.

II

Before considering these recent times and the later reformists, it is time to look at the leading neutralists. This latter group was more diverse and overlapping, but two main sorts may be distinguished.

First, there were those who saw that if the subject were to deal historically with the variables which were the concern of economics, then it must be inherently quantitative. As Clapham put it, 'every economic historian should have

[34] Ibid., p. 232.
[35] D. Cannadine, 'The Present and the Past in the English Industrial Revolution, 1880–1980', *Past and Present* 103 (1984), p. 138.

acquired . . . the habit of asking in relation to any institution, policy, group or movement the questions: how large? how long? how often? how representative?'.[36] The novelty of this approach deserves emphasis. The compilation of numerical data has, as shown earlier, a respectably long pedigree, from Fleetwood and Anderson to McCulloch, Tooke and Newmarch, and Thorold Rogers.[37] But none of the pioneering generation of economic historians used that data to answer the type of questions posed by Clapham. Rogers' use of the wage and price data which he collected was narrow and essentially antiquarian; and such works of his as *The Economic Interpretation of History* and *England's Industrial and Commercial Supremacy* are wholly devoid of any sense of the quantitative. Likewise, although some figures are scattered about their pages, neither Cunningham nor even Unwin, and certainly not Ashley, ever used them in any systematic fashion to analyse the phenomena they investigated.

The extent to which the new quantitative approach also implied the conscious use of economic theory varied greatly. There can be no doubt that it was Marshall's neo-classical economics, with its absorption of the marginalist revolution and the mathematical treatment of variables, that opened up the possibility of using a general framework of economic questions and numerical data in the analysis of historical phenomena. The emergence of a type of economic history which was tied neither to the dogmatic and bankrupt political economy of the English school nor to the ineffective historical economics of the German school was thus permitted. Permission was not, however, readily or easily translated into practice, for reasons already indicated.[38] The conflict between Marshall and Cunningham; the subsequent indifference to history on the part of economic theorists; and the continuing hostility to economics on the part of the reformist historians:

[36] *Encyclopaedia of the Social Sciences* v (1931), p. 328.
[37] See above, pp. 25–6, 38, 54.
[38] See above, pp. 45–7.

all contributed to the continuance in Britain of the gulf between economics and economic history. So the use of economics in the examination of the past was, for long, confined to that general framework which allowed simply the posing of broad economic questions. Clapham provided the crucial link with Marshall, but his own use of theory was very limited and never extended beyond a broad and general Marshallian framework. Indeed, in 1922, he expressed his dissatisfaction with the shortcomings of the economists' tools in a celebrated and influential attack upon economic abstractions as 'empty boxes'.[39] Moreover, his inaugural lecture in 1929, as the first occupant of the new chair of economic history at Cambridge, though stressing that the economic historian had to be 'a measurer above other historians', again referred to the economist's 'emptier categories'[40] and contained none of those exhortations to use economic theory which were later to become common form in such inaugural pronouncements.

By far the best survey and critical appreciation of Clapham's works is that by Harry Court, originally buried in 1956 in the tomb of a Festschrift but happily reprinted in his *Scarcity and Choice in History*.[41] There is no need to repeat it here. Today, those three massive volumes of Clapham's *Economic History of Modern Britain*, published between 1926 and 1938, totalling over 1,700 pages, and reprinted at various times up to 1964, may seem almost unreadable. Yet, it is well to remember that, in its day, the work as a whole was an incomparable achievement; that despite the static nature of its analysis and absence of concern with the causes of economic change, it remains a valuable repository of information; and that it represented a formidable contrast to the emotionally

---

[39] 'Of Empty Economic Boxes', *Economic Journal* XXXII (1922), pp. 305–14.
[40] 'The Study of Economic History', reprinted in Harte (ed.), *Study*, pp. 67–8.
[41] Originally published in J. T. Lambie (ed.), *Architects and Craftsmen in History* (Tübingen, 1956); reprinted in Court (ed.), *Scarcity and Choice*, pp. 141–50.

charged accounts of the industrial revolution in Britain penned by the reformists. Clapham's attack on their approach had been launched on a small scale in his 1912 review of the Hammonds' *Village Labourer*.[42] It was then obliquely re-asserted in the preface to volume I of the *Economic History of Modern Britain*. It gave rise to the well-known debate about the standard of living of workers during the industrial revolution, a debate which went rumbling on, as 'optimists' versus 'pessimists', for years and years, pausing only for a brief intermission during World War II, and not apparently expiring until the 1970s—though it may prove to have further life in it yet. With its nature I am not here concerned. What is worthy of emphasis, however, is Clapham's insistence upon a balanced presentation of findings, obtained by asking broadly economic questions, aided by numbers and without the prior assumption that capitalism was a phenomenon conducive to increased misery for the many and, therefore, of itself demanding reproach or reform.

It is in this sense that his approach may be called neutralist, as distinct from reformist. He gave voice to these views in 1921 in his *Economic Development of France and Germany 1815–1914*. He reminded his readers in the Introduction that 'what is called capitalism had long existed in Western Europe. In one or other of its forms, agrarian, commercial or industrial, it is as old as civilization'.[43] At the end, having demonstrated that the nineteenth century had brought a higher standard of living to the workers of these two countries, he noted that the advances had not been wiped out by the rising prices of 1901–14 and concluded:

... it is impossible to argue that the solid economic gains which the average hand worker had made during the great peace of the nineteenth century were seriously threatened. A purely historical

[42] *Econ. Jnl.* XXII (1912), pp. 248–55.
[43] *Economic Development of France and Germany, 1815–1914* (Cambridge, 1921; 4th edn. 1936, repr. 1945), p. 2.

conclusion this, which involves no blessing and no cursing of the social system of Europe in the first decade of the twentieth century.[44]

Despite the much greater popular appeal of the reformists, Clapham was not wholly alone, in the early decades of the century, amongst economic historians favouring the detached economic approach. E. C. K. Gonner's *Common Land and Inclosure* (1912) examined a heavily charged subject, in its manifestations from the fifteenth to the eighteenth centuries, with a dispassionate air which earned Clapham's approval: 'Professor Gonner is everything that Mr. and Mrs. Hammond are not, detached, not easy to read, fond of qualifying clauses, formally economic, given to maps and statistics ... '.[45] Gonner was also everything that they were not, in a different sense, for he was Professor of Economic Science at Liverpool University, an editor of Ricardo, and a government adviser on statistical and economic matters. His book on enclosures was also, as Clapham observed, 'bloodless as a Board of Trade return'.[46] So it is the Hammonds' view which has survived in the popular historical consciousness: only bloodless experts want bloodless history.

Another massive achievement of detached observation, dating from these early decades and which is often overlooked in recitals of economic historiography, has a title so forbidding as admittedly to scare away any but the dedicated expert. *The Constitution and Finance of English, Scottish and Irish Joint-Stock Companies to 1720* came out in three volumes in 1910–12. Its author, W. R. Scott, was, like Gonner, an economist with historical interests. Elected to the Adam Smith Chair of Political Economy at Glasgow University in 1915, he served as President of the Economic History Society, 1927–40. He was

---

[44] Ibid., p. 407.

[45] *Econ. Jnl.* XXII (1912), p. 252.

[46] Ibid. Professor Sir Edward Carter Kersey Gonner, CBE, KCB was *inter alia* a member of the Royal Commission on Shipping Conferences. His knighthood came in 1921. *Common Land and Inclosure* was reprinted, with an Introduction by G. E. Mingay, in 1966.

most unusual amongst academic economists and historians in also being a practical businessman, for he long directed the affairs of the family milling business in Northern Ireland.[47] To many, he is perhaps best remembered for his biographical work on Adam Smith.[48] But his remarkable research in early business organization not only provided a detailed examination of the history from 1553 to 1720 of the joint-stock method of raising capital but also extended into public finance and the trade cycle. His work asked economic questions, provided and used statistics, and had nothing whatever to do with the seductive appeal of social tragedy, middle-class social guilt, and reforming the present.

The economists' approach to history took a further step forward with the work of a later leading neutralist, T. S. Ashton. As Richard Sayers remarked in his sympathetic account of Ashton's life, 'more than anyone else, more even than Clapham, he made economic history the economist's history'.[49] Ashton continued and substantially extended Clapham's emphasis on the necessarily quantitative nature of the subject. His last major work, *Economic Fluctuations in England 1700–1800* (1959), used statistics to illuminate the cycles of economic growth in eighteenth-century England in a manner far removed from anything that Clapham achieved. Furthermore, his treatment of the economic past was informed by a much greater use and understanding of Marshallian economics. This derived from his having read political economy and history at Manchester University; from his having taught currency and public finance in the economics department there for over twenty years; and from an apprenticeship in research which resulted in his very first published work in 1914 being, like his last, an exercise in the

---

[47] J. H. Clapham, 'William Robert Scott, 1868–1940', *Proceedings of the British Academy* XXVI (1940), pp. 479–87.

[48] *Adam Smith as Student and Professor* (Glasgow, 1937).

[49] R. S. Sayers, 'Thomas Southcliffe Ashton, 1889–1968', *Proc. Brit. Acad.* LVI (1970), p. 281.

numerical analysis of a problem presented in Marshallian terms.[50] Between those first and last publications, he made his reputation as an economic historian by a series of books on English industry in the eighteenth century. That which reached the widest public, and also stamped him clearly as Clapham's successor in opposition to the reformists' views on the industrial revolution, could not have been more of a contrast in size to Clapham's massive trilogy. *The Industrial Revolution 1760–1830* (1948), published four years after his appointment to the chair of economic history at LSE, is a remarkable feat of compression, packing into some 160 pages of octavo format a remarkably lucid descriptive analysis of seventy years during which 'the face of England changed'.[51] Its concluding words stand in stark opposition to the guilt-laden sentiments of the reformists.

The central problem of the age was how to feed and clothe and employ generations of children outnumbering by far those of any earlier time . . . If England had remained a nation of cultivators and craftsmen, she could hardly have escaped the same fate [as Ireland] . . . she was delivered, not by her rulers, but by those who, seeking no doubt their own narrow ends, had the wit and resource to devise new instruments of production and new methods of administering industry.[52]

Having a few pages earlier commented that 'a statistician of repute' had stated that 'by the early years of the nineteenth century the standard of life of the British worker had been forced down to Asiatic levels',[53] Ashton ended his book with these challenging words:

[50] T. S. Ashton and S. J. Chapman, 'The Size of Businesses, mainly in the Textile Industries', *Journal of the Royal Statistical Society* New Ser. LXXVII (1913–14), pp. 465–549.
[51] *The Industrial Revolution 1760–1830* (Oxford, 1948), p. 1. The book was originally published in the Home University Library series and the page references here given refer to that edition.
[52] Ibid., p. 161.
[53] Ibid., p. 157.

There are today on the plains of India and China men and women, plague-ridden and hungry, living lives little better, to outward appearance, than those of the cattle that toil with them by day and share their places of sleep by night. Such Asiatic standards, and such unmechanized horrors, are the lot of those who increase their numbers without passing through an industrial revolution.[54]

The challenging words certainly kept going the 'optimists' versus 'pessimists' debate. A few years later, Ashton published similar observations in a book edited by F. A. Hayek, *Capitalism and the Historians* (1954). There he cannot but seem a partisan rather than a neutralist. Furthermore, as Hayek's *Road to Serfdom* of 1944 had acquired something of the status of an election document of the Tory party, immediately preceding, as it did, the General Election of 1945, Ashton came to be regarded as more than simply an 'optimist' in a particular academic debate. More to the immediate point, however, the whole concluding passage of *The Industrial Revolution* presented an essentially counterfactual argument, apparently neutralist in its use of simple economic variables, though evoking the human spirit in its celebration of an achievement, which was of course capitalist in nature, as a response to the pressure of mounting population. It also shot a glancing blow ('not by her rulers') at one of Ashton's favourite targets: the role of the state.

In this he was undoubtedly much influenced by Unwin. Both came from lower middle class Nonconformist backgrounds in the industrial north-west of England. Both got to university by hard work and scholarships. Neither was afflicted by Public Schools, Anglicanism, Christian Socialism, or middle-class social guilt. Neither had much faith in the economic achievements of state power; both believed that historians were over-impressed by it. Unwin, a lifelong free-trader, had a poor opinion of government economic policy and its supposed basis in preconceived economic strategy. He deplored 'the tendency to overestimate the active part which

[54] *The Industrial Revolution*, p. 161.

wise forethought and the deliberate pursuit of clear ideas has played in the economic history of nations'.[55] Conversely, he was consistently impressed by human achievements secured in voluntary associations for common ends. He was instrumental in getting Ashton onto the Manchester staff in 1921 and his ideas found a receptive response in Ashton's own brand of Manchester liberalism, sturdy, humane, unphilosophical, and unpretentious. A photograph of Unwin surveyed Ashton's doings—through a haze of cigarette smoke—in the latter's room at LSE. One of the results is that, in Ashton's version of economic history, the state seems hardly to exist. What mattered was 'the economy'. The price of his great achievement in ensuring that British economic historians should seek to discover how the economy worked and moved was the near disappearance of governments as agents in social and economic life. Sharing Unwin's scepticism about the efficacy of government economic policy, he ignored it. Thereby, he totally reversed the thrust of the sort of economic history pioneered by Cunningham.

If, in Ashton's hands, the linkage between economics and economic history in Britain was thus strengthened, the second sort of neutralism operated in the opposite way and tended to keep the subject more in the domain of the historian. Its chief representative, from the same generation as Ashton, was a man who, appropriately for his interests, was successively Professor of Economic History at Oxford (1931–43) and Regius Professor of Modern History at Cambridge (1943–7): G. N. (later Sir George) Clark.

After a brilliant performance at Oxford as an undergraduate, Clark moved on to the study of European history in the seventeenth century and especially to Holland and Anglo-Dutch relations. His *The Dutch Alliance and the War against French Trade* (1923) was an unusual mixture of political and commercial history. Clark was essentially an historian with a remarkably wide range of interests, which happened to

[55] Tawney (ed.), *Studies in Economic History: Collected Papers of George Unwin*, p. 158.

include the economic, rather than a specialist versed in economic matters. This notable width of learning made itself evident
in *The Seventeenth Century* (1929), rightly described as 'a
most precocious work'.[56] It was certainly then unusual for an
array of topics—from Armies to Education and from Frontiers
to Philosophy—to be treated as they were and not least for the
sequence to start with Population, followed by three chapters
on economic matters. The same comprehensive embrace was
evident in *The Later Stuarts 1660–1714* (1934). This was
volume 10 of the Oxford History of England of which he was
the general editor; and it came out three years after he had
been appointed to the new economic history chair at Oxford.
It cannot be said to have contributed very much specifically to
economic history, though it did maintain some integration of
the commerical and the political in its treatment of foreign
policy and overseas relations. This type of integration was a
characteristic feature of Clark's work and is reminiscent to
some extent of Cunningham; it has been continued by later
historians in a not dissimilar mould, for example, Charles
Wilson.[57] Having come to occupy the economic history chair,
Clark signalled the appointment by preparing his *Guide to
English Commercial Statistics 1696–1782* (1938). A very useful
compilation it is, but two points need to be made about it.
First, it largely consists of an appendix of documents and a
catalogue of statistical material, both prepared by others
under Clark's direction; his own contribution is confined to an
account of how the data came to be collected and to a brief
discussion of their value. Second, he himself never, thereafter,
made any significant economic use of those data in examining
the economic history of England. His main subsequent contribution to that subject was contained in his companion volume
to Ashton's in the Home University Library series (which he
edited), *The Wealth of England 1496–1760* (1946).

[56] Geoffrey Parker, 'George Norman Clark, 1890–1979', *Proc. Brit. Acad.* LXVI
(1980), p. 414.
[57] Who was also Professor of Modern History at Cambridge, from 1965 to 1979.

In his younger days Clark had been a Fabian socialist and a supporter of the Labour party.[58] So he might well have become a candidate for membership of the reformist category of economic historians. But after the 1926 general strike his abandonment of that political cause was as evident as the neutralist stance of such economic history as he wrote. It was urbane, clear, bland; not praising, not condemning; neither troubled by concern for the present nor made rigorous by the application of economic analysis to the past. Both in his inaugural lecture of 1932 and in his *Wealth of England* in 1946 he stressed the interdependence of all sorts of history. Economic history he saw in 1932 as 'an abstract kind of history related to the full and concrete history somewhat as economic theory is related to the full and concrete life of the community'.[59] At the end of the 1946 survey he reiterated that there was 'no firm borderline marking off economic affairs from politics, religion, science, education, and all the other aspects of human life'.[60] Sensible sentiments, no doubt, and worth saying. But unsupported by any examination of possible interrelationships or of the problems posed by contrasting methods of enquiry, they could hardly satisfy the intellectually hungry. Characteristically, the activity of writing and reading the *Wealth of England* is described, both at the start and at the finish of the work, by the verb 'to trace'. The first sentence tells the reader that 'economic history traces through the past the matters with which economics is concerned'. At the end the reader is invited to 'look back over the changes we have traced'.[61] Not analysing, not using economics, not posing economic questions, not demanding to know how long, how much, or how representative: but tracing. This was indeed the historian's route to the neutralist position.

---

[58] Parker, 'George Norman Clark', p. 412; A. J. P. Taylor, *A Personal History* (1983; paperback edn., 1984), pp. 81, 102.
[59] G. N. Clark, 'The Study of Economic History' in Harte (ed.), *Study*, pp. 85–6.
[60] *Wealth of England* (Oxford, 1946), p. 190.
[61] Ibid., pp. 1 and 190.

III

The very diversity of approaches to the economic past, far from impeding a growing interest in the subject during the inter-war years, probably helped it. New students took up the study of economic history; more books were written about it; new appointments were made in the universities. As expansion proceeded, so did the boundaries of the twofold categorization of reformists and neutralists become blurred.

Some on the boundaries seem to resist instant classification. One such was Ephraim Lipson. His *chef d'œuvre, The Economic History of England*, published in three volumes between 1915 and 1930, went through many editions and was for long the standard text on pre-industrial England. In its systematization, it apparently owed a good deal to German historicist influences. Four stages of evolution were detected in the history of industrial organization: the household, the guild, the domestic, and the factory. The two-and-a-half centuries, 1550–1800, were comprehensively labelled as 'The Age of Mercantilism' and seen as a phase in the continuous working out of two 'factors' in the making of English society: co-operation and individualism. Medieval England was an example of the former; the nineteenth century and *laissez-faire* typified the latter. In between, 'the Age of Mercantilism was one of transition'.[62] Lipson's volumes do not belong to the reformist category; but neither do they ask the quantitative or economic questions associated with Clapham or Ashton. They have little to say of such matters as capital accumulation or population change. But they are full of information and they show a great knowledge of printed (though not of manuscript) contemporary sources. Lipson, who got Firsts in both parts of the History Tripos at Cambridge, became Reader in Economic History at Oxford, but in 1931 was passed over for the newly created chair in the subject in favour of G. N. Clark. He

---

[62] *The Economic History of England* (4th edn.) II, p. ii.

played a major part in the founding of the Economic History Society and was the first joint-editor, along with Tawney, of its journal *The Economic History Review* from 1926 to 1934. His rejection in 1931, however, hit him hard. A sensitive man who suffered from a physical deformity, he quitted Oxford shortly after the announcement of Clark's election to the chair and rarely returned thereafter.[63]

Of far greater lasting consequence for the subject was the growing tendency to present it not just as a sort of history which dealt with economic matters but as a member of the new and flourishing family of the social sciences. This may, in part, have represented a conscious distancing from the conflict between reformists and neutralists. But it also drew upon a growing appreciation that the economic past was too interesting to be left simply to historians with an interest in economics or to economists disposed to desert the present. A wider vision demanded the contributions of anthropology and sociology, as well as that awareness of older and different legal systems which had been brought in by Maine, Maitland, and Vinogradoff. So it is not coincidental that it was from economic historians whose chief concern was with earlier periods of history that the call came for integration with the other social sciences.

Inaugural lectures often provided occasions for such calls. Tawney, in 1932, not only emphasized that history was in his view concerned with 'the life of society', but also played some homage to the desirability of studying similar phenomena in diverse societies. His advice to the student of European industrial civilization that he should read Raymond Firth on the Maori was more than a passing politeness to a then rising young lecturer in anthropology in the same institution.[64] More specific and sustained references to the social sciences

[63] For comments and reminisences of Lipson, see the entry (by Herbert Heaton) in the *DNB* and also T. C. Barker, 'The Beginnings of the Economic History Society', *Econ. Hist. Rev.* 2nd Ser. xxx (1977), pp. 9–13.

[64] Tawney in Harte (ed.), *Study*, pp. 96, 100.

came from Eileen Power, a Cambridge medievalist, who joined the staff at LSE in 1921 and was appointed to a new chair in economic history there in 1932.[65] In her inaugural of 1933, she set out deliberately to build bridges between the disparate disciplines which converged upon the subject. 'The historians', she observed, 'are so hard on the sociologists, and the economists so rude to the historians, that any improvement in the world of social science seems almost beyond human hope'. She asserted her more sanguine belief, however, that anthropologists, sociologists, economists, and historians were alive to the need for an integration of their labours and an understanding of their aims and methods. Ranging critically through Marx, Weber, and Sombart, she made an eloquent plea for the use of a 'genuinely scientific method of abstraction and comparison' in the study of medieval history.[66]

In practice, Eileen Power's published works revealed only a very limited use of such techniques. Her very real gift for popularization exhibited in *Medieval People* (1924, and later much reprinted in paperback) unhappily identified her with a cosy sort of social history, short on the analytical and strong on the picturesque.[67] Only in her later work, mainly on the medieval wool trade, did she begin to show the fruits of trying to put history into the context of the social sciences, efforts which were brought to a close by her sudden and early death in 1940. A far more sustained advocacy and, to some extent, practice of the integration of economic history with the social sciences came from her husband, M. M. Postan, formerly her research assistant, whom she married in 1937.

Of all who practised economic history in Britain, Sir Michael Moissey Postan was undoubtedly one of the more influential in helping to orientate the subject in the direction

[65] See C. W. Webster, 'Eileen Power, 1889–1940', *Econ. Jnl.* L (1940), pp. 561–72.
[66] 'On Medieval History as a Social Study', reprinted in Harte (ed.), *Study*, pp. 111, 125.
[67] What might be called the 'it-was-on-just-such-a-day-as-this' school.

of the social sciences. Coming to England from his native Russia, via various parts of Europe, and graduating at LSE in 1924, he succeeded Clapham as Professor of Economic History at Cambridge in 1938. Perhaps because of the combination of a cosmopolitan educational background and graduation at a school avowedly dedicated to the social sciences, he was one of the very few economic historians in Britain to concern themselves with methodological issues. In a series of articles, between 1934 and 1969, he sketched out a view of the nature of economic history and of its relations to history and economics which committed him to an almost Comtean view of its social science function.[68] He attacked conventional historiography ('Most orthodox historians cling to the belief that their real business is to study facts'),[69] thus ensuring that some of his more conventional colleagues amongst Cambridge historians regarded him as a charlatan.[70] He combined a sympathetic view of both economics and sociology with a sharply critical eye for the more dogmatic claims of economic theorists or the grandiose generalizations of some sociologists. But he retained, throughout, an approach which was usefully summarized in this remark from his inaugural lecture of 1938: 'Where the historian shows his scientific preoccupations, and qualifies for membership of the social sciences, is in concentrating the study of his individual subject on its relevance to general and theoretical problems'.[71]

Despite some sympathies with the modern political Left,[72] neither from his methodological utterances nor from his substantive work on medieval (and modern) economic history

[68] Gathered together in *Fact and Relevance: Essays in the Historical Method* (Cambridge, 1971).

[69] Ibid., p. 48.

[70] One was far more likely to meet economists and social scientists than historians at the hospitable Postan house in Cambridge. And it is perhaps hardly surprising to read that the judgement on Postan by one fellow Cambridge historian, Edward Welbourne, 'cannot be reported', even by another Cambridge historian, Maurice Cowling, in his *Religion and Public Doctrine* (Cambridge, 1980), p. 69.

[71] 'The Historical Method in Social Science' in Harte (ed.), *Study*, p. 138.

[72] See 'Hugh Gaitskell: Political and Intellectual Progress', reprinted in *Fact and Relevance*, pp. 169–82.

could a real case be made for putting Postan in the reformist category. Although the sort of economic history written by Postan or Power differed from that written by Lipson and both differed again from that of Clapham, Ashton, or Clark, all in effect reinforced the neutralist category, in the sense of not offering a set of messages, for the purpose of attacking a capitalist past, in the name of reforming the present.

6

Upswing and Downturn

Of all varieties of history the economic is the most fundamental. Not the most important: foundations exist to carry
better things.

J. H. Clapham, *A Concise Economic History of Britain* (1949)

I

THE foundation of the Economic History Society in 1926 and
the publication of the first issue of the *Economic History Review*
in 1927 came at a time when, despite the pre-war appointments and enthusiasm, the subject had only a rather slender
hold in the formal establishment of British universities.
Indeed, it was apparently less secure than it had been. By the
time that the Society's inaugural meeting was held, in the
summer of 1926, the first two professors of the subject, George
Unwin at Manchester and Lilian Knowles at LSE, had both
died and no successors had been appointed; Oxford and
Cambridge had yet to make such appointments. As already
indicated in Chapter 4, one of the legacies of Marshall's
victory over Cunningham at Cambridge was a continued
distancing of the emergent subject from economic theory. Its
uneasy lodgement in university departments of history not
only reinforced that isolation but also ensured that it was
regarded warily by many orthodox historians. It was hardly
surprising that the formation of the Economic History Society,
as is evident from Professor Barker's account, did not proceed
in an atmosphere of total harmony and unanimity.[1] Relations

[1] Barker, 'Beginnings of the Economic History Society', pp. 6–16.

between Tawney and Lipson were equivocal; both Clapham himself and the Cambridge economics establishment held aloof; there were real doubts about the ability of the Society to survive; and for some time its financial situation certainly remained parlous. It drew its sustenance from extra-university enthusiasm, from the devoted secretarial work of Eileen Power, and from the growing reputation of the *Economic History Review*.

Movements in the membership figures of the Society, and hence sales figures of the *Review*, provide some indication of the subject's popularity. Between 1927 and 1939 total paid-up membership had risen by 14 per cent, from 611 to 699. The totals conceal, however, a fall in individual subscriptions by 8 per cent (from 487 to 449), effectively outweighed by a rise of 102 per cent in library sales (from 124 to 250).[2] The inference to be drawn from this would seem to be that universities and colleges, at home and abroad, together with a few other educational institutions, were impressed by the new journal (it expanded to two issues in 1931), but that amongst individual scholars, teachers, or amateurs of the subject the initial burst of enthusiasm could not be fully maintained. Numbers of publications on British economic and social history, as listed in the annual bibliographies published in the *Review*, showed a drop of some 19 per cent for numbers of books and a rise of 64 per cent in articles.[3] Again, this testifies to a growing volume of scholarly research but is hardly suggestive of a startling spurt of interest. The war years 1939–45 inevitably brought a decline in all indices: total membership dropped 15 per cent from 699 to 594; annual publications also fell sharply.

An astonishing surge in the popularity of the subject followed in the first three post-war decades. From 1945 to its high point in 1977 total membership of the Economic History

[2] The relevant data are provided in Barker, Table 1, p. 2.

[3] N. B. Harte, 'Trends in Publications on the Economic and Social History of Great Britain and Ireland, 1925–74', *Econ. Hist. Rev.* 2nd Ser. xxx (1977), Table 1, p. 24. The figures given above relate to the changes between the averages for 1925–7 and 1937–9.

Society and sales of the *Economic History Review* rose to 5,126, an increase of 763 per cent. Within this total, individual subscriptions rose by 613 per cent, library and trade sales by 1,004 per cent.[4] Universities, colleges, polytechnics, and schools in the UK and in many parts of the world, stocked their library shelves with volume upon volume of a journal which had become an essential element in the scholarly study of this booming academic subject. Even these rates of growth understate: the two issues a year of 1931 became three in 1948 and four in 1971; moreover, they grew fatter the while, the 350 pages per year of 1949–50 rising to a peak in the mid-1970s when some 750 pages of concentrated economic history scholarship were delivered to subscribers every year. University appointments followed a similar course of increase. At the outbreak of war in 1939 the subject had four professors (two at LSE and one each at Oxford and Cambridge).[5] By the 1970s the four had become twenty-four.[6] With a parallel expansion in supporting staffs and in research students, books and articles proliferated accordingly. In the 1930s the number of items listed in the annual bibliographies of the *Review* averaged about 45 books and 55 articles; by the early 1970s the corresponding figures were approximately 285 and 1,025.[7]

Propulsion for this rocket came from a variety of fuels. Not all were domestic in origin. The vigour of the German historicists had naturally led to the first of the specialized journals; the *Vierteljahrschrift für Sozial und Wirtschaftsgeschichte* began in 1903 and was for a while the only outlet for learned articles in the subject. In France the *Revue d'histoire économique et sociale* started in 1913. So the *Economic History Review's* beginning in 1927 was, to some extent, a belated British catching-up on

[4] Barker, 'Beginnings', p. 2; and figures kindly provided by the Assistant Secretary of the Economics History Society.

[5] Tawney and Power at LSE; Clark and Postan at Oxford and Cambridge respectively.

[6] The total, which naturally fluctuated during the decade, includes both established chairs and *ad hominem* professorships. If separate social history posts are included the figure becomes 28.

[7] Harte, 'Trends', p. 24.

continental European endeavour. Its subsequent boom proceeded at the same time as that of the *Journal of Economic History* in the USA, the organ of the Economic History Association which started life there in 1941. The number of its subscribers multiplied with similar rapidity from about 400 in 1941 to some 3,600 in the mid-1970s. It likewise grew fat, becoming a four-issue annual, totalling over 1,000 pages, before the end of that decade. The appearance in 1929 of *Annales*, which later adopted the comprehensive subtitle, *Économies, sociétés, civilisations*, had ushered in a new sort of French concern for the economic and social past. In 1953 Swedish enterprise created the more conventional *Scandinavian Economic History Review* which was published in English. These, and other journals elsewhere, testified to a far more than merely British upswing in the subject. Conferences also multiplied and in 1960 came the first International Conference of Economic History, held in Stockholm, and the foundation of the International Economic History Association.

More immediately pertinent and powerful were those sources of propulsion generated at home in Britain. One was the raising of the school leaving age and the initial expansion of higher education in the UK, which was further sustained by the Robbins Report of 1963. Within the big package, certain subjects gained disproportionately whilst others correspondingly lost. Among the former were the social sciences, with economics and economic history well to the fore; among the latter, Latin and Greek. The numbers taking the subject called English Economic History or Economic and Social History at O level in the GCE examinations showed a higher than average rate of increase from the 1950s to about 1970; those at A level followed a similar path, reaching a peak in 1971.[8] If interest in the subject was thus being furthered in

[8] Figures kindly provided by the Department of Education and Science and originally used in my *What has Happened to Economic History?* (Cambridge, 1972), in which see pp. 2–6 for an indication of sundry snags in the use of these figures, which also apply to the published data in HMSO, *Statistics of Education*. But the broad relative trends are almost certainly correct.

schools, it was given a boost in the upper reaches of the educational hierarchy by the setting up in 1965 of the Social Science Research Council. In 1968, economic and social history jointly became one of the fourteen or so subjects accorded the dignity of a separate advisory committee within the Council's administrative structure. Although not one of the biggest recipients of the Council's budget—economics generally received the largest annual share—quite substantial sums were allocated to finance postgraduate studentships and/or research grants in economic and social history. By the mid-1970s the subject was annually receiving over 100 postgraduate awards as well as research grants totalling around £200,000. These figures represented approximately 8 per cent of the total number of postgraduate awards and of the total value of research grants made by the Council.

Beyond the immediacy of SSRC grants and awards there lay such manifestations of the age as the Education Act of 1944, the Beveridge Plan, the commitment to full employment policies, and all those hopes for recovery, renewal, and reform which brought in the Labour government in 1945 and which were continued by the broad social and economic consensus imprecisely labelled Butskellism. As an adjunct to those goals of endeavour, the task of extending and deepening our knowledge of the economic past seemed entirely pertinent. Its potential usefulness as a guide to future progress—so nicely lauded by Cunningham in his SPCK pamphlet of 1919[9]—gained a renewed momentum. Clapham added his weighty influence in pronouncing it to be 'the most fundamental' sort of history. And the emphasis on British economic recovery endowed it with a further claim as the more 'relevant' variety. If, in the 1930s, the impact of depression and unemployment had turned some students away from the political and constitutional history which still formed the staple diet of orthodox history teaching in Britain and towards

[9] See epigraph to Chapter 5.

economic history, so the very different post-war years strongly reinforced this tendency. The emphasis of interest shifted accordingly. Whereas during the inter-war years concern with distributive justice, as it seemed to the reformists, loomed large, post-war recovery stimulated a new fascination with the historical problems of production, technical change, and, above all, economic growth.

II

The great boom could not last. Soon it began to go the way of all such phenomena: retardation appeared in some indicators, absolute decline in others. At the lower end of the educational scale there was, interestingly enough, no apparent indication of downturn. Over the twelve years between the two 3-year averages of 1968–70 and 1980–2, entries for the subject English Economic History at O level rose by 51 per cent.[10] This was significantly more than the equivalent increase in total entries for all subjects which was 39 per cent; and very much more than the corresponding figure for History which was barely 1 per cent.[11]

These figures should not, however, be taken at face value. Three points need to be made about them. First, the two subjects, i.e. Economic History and History, are not discrete statistical entities; some examining boards include economic and social history within their history syllabuses. The significance of this seems to be unmeasurable. Second, economic history at O level is generally thought to have been regarded for some time as rather a soft option, both in schools and in colleges of further education; entrants from the latter (where the subject is popular) are included in the statistics. Consequently, the figures may well be testifying more to the hopes of

[10] Calculated from figures given in R. G. Wilson and J. F. Hadwin, 'Economic and Social History at Advanced Level', *Econ. Hist. Rev.* 2nd Ser. xxxviii (1985), Table 1, p. 551. They rose from an average of 32,803 in 1968–70 to 49,438 in 1980–2. The authors of the article incorrectly put that change at 68 per cent (p. 559).
[11] Ibid., Table 1.

poorer candidates than to the enthusiasm of the more able. On the other hand, the pass rate for economic history—in 1968 only 47.8 per cent as compared with 55.5 per cent for history, thus seemingly confirming this supposition—had so improved that by 1982 there was little to chose between the two subjects.[12] Third, the rate of increase in this period, 1968–70 to 1980–2, was almost certainly much less than in the corresponding preceding period, 1958–60 to 1970–2.[13] This is not inherently surprising, but it does suggest that, although absolute numbers have continued to grow, retardation has set in even at O level.

Move up the educational scale, and deceleration becomes decline. The A-level entries for economic history reached their peak in 1971. From then on, the downturn becomes very evident. Taking again the averages for 1968–70 and 1980–2, the fall was −25 per cent. The ratio of A-level to O-level candidates gives some indication of the subject's appeal to those who may go on to university. This settled down at around 15 per cent in the 1960s, with a high point in 1968. Again using the same three-year averages, 1968–70 to 1980–2, the ratio more than halves from 15.4 to 7.4. Comparison with the numbers of candidates for the history papers shows that, over the same period, the 24.9 per cent fall in ecomomic history was paralleled by a small rise, 5.1 per cent, in history. Total entries, meanwhile, rose by 36.8 per cent. So history was a relative loser and economic history a clear absolute loser. Furthermore, level of performance, as measured by the number of A and B grades in A-level results, reveals economic history as a magnet for lower quality candidates. The percentage of A and B grades in 1968–70 averaged 22.9 for history and 12.6 for economic history. And it worsened: in 1982 it had

[12] Ibid., Table 1.
[13] On pre-1968 figures, see n. 8 above. The equivalent increase over the period 1958–60 to 1970–2 appears to have been 228 per cent but this unquestionably exaggerates the true rate of increase because some of the earlier data are incomplete. Nevertheless, it seems highly probable that the rate of increase was significantly higher than in the later period.

fallen slightly for history to 22.1, a drop of 3.5 per cent, while for economic history it had fallen to 10.7, a drop of 15.1 per cent.[14]

Neither the ratio of A- to O-level candidates nor the relative quality of A-level performance can provide more than very rough indications of interest in the subject at university level. Many undergraduates, and indeed graduates, have gone on to embrace the study of economic history without having taken it at A level. Moreover, experience of a wholly unquantifiable nature suggests that in economic history, as in economics, having studied the subject at A level can even be disadvantageous. To meet the demand, much poor teaching by persons ill-qualified in the subject has gone on in schools and colleges of various sorts. But the statistics do at least provide some measure of support for the subjective impression that economic history has tended to attract too many undergraduates of only mediocre ability; and that too many of the better research students go elsewhere.

There are also some quite other signs of both failing appeal and weakening support in the higher reaches of education and intellectual activity. According to a survey carried out in 1982, a score of full-time university posts in the subject were lost in Britain between 1978 and 1982.[15] That boom in professorships likewise began to wane as chairs were left unfilled or fewer *ad hominem* professorships granted. In some universities, small and vulnerable economic history departments have ceased to exist. The number of SSRC postgraduate studentships for economic history fell dramatically from its high point of 107 in the mid-1970s to a mere 47 in 1981-2, representing a fall in relative importance in the total of such grants from 8 per cent to 5 per cent. Reorganization of the SSRC (transmuted into ESRC—Economic and Social Research Council —because of a ministerial dislike of the notion of 'social

[14] All figures in the above paragraph have been calculated from Wilson and Hadwin, 'Economic History at Advanced Level', Tables 1 and 2, pp. 551-2.
[15] Ibid., p. 548, n. 1.

sciences') brought the abolition in 1983 of the separate Economic and Social History Committee. Down-graded in status, the interests of the subject were then dispersed over two new committees; Economic Affairs; and Industry and Employment. Finally, and perhaps most suggestive of the subject's decline, at least in the way that it had been presented in Britain, membership of the Economic History Society and the circulation of the *Economic History Review* have fallen steadily from the 1970s peak, dropping 16 per cent between 1977 and 1984.[16] The *Review's* size has likewise been subjected to slimming; the 750 pages of the mid-1970s contracted to around 650 by the early 1980s. In contrast, its US counterpart, the *Journal of Economic History*, although also showing signs of slackening momentum, dropped only 3 per cent in total paid circulation over the same period and maintained, or even slightly increased, its 1000-page size.

III

This whole sequence—early enthusiasm, inter-war establishment, post-war boom, and then decline—is intimately linked with the rise, persistence, and crumbling of that posture of opposition which has been so integral a feature of the study of the economic past in Britain. Smith and Millar in opposition to orthodox historiography; Cliffe Leslie, Cunningham, and Ashley in opposition to orthodox political economy; the reformists in opposition to the capitalist past and present; the neutralists in opposition to the reformists: the battle was long-enduring and certainly offered intellectual stimuli. But relief was at hand. In the quarter of a century or so after World War II, the study of economic history in Britain acquired an orthodoxy of its own and became respectable. And respectability is a sure symptom of declining vitality, even if not quite the first sign of rigor mortis.

Respectable orthodoxy was achieved by various routes. The

[16] See n. 4 above.

broad highway of the neutralists was of central importance. By the time that the subject began its rapid post-war expansion, neutralists of sundry sorts occupied all the active chairs of economic history in Britain. To such very different neutralists as Ashton and Postan, at LSE and Cambridge respectively, were added Arthur Redford at Manchester (in 1945) and W. H. B. Court at Birmingham (in 1947); at Oxford, after Clark's move to the chair of modern history at Cambridge, the brief tenure of the chair by W. K. Hancock (1944–9)[17] was followed by that of H. J. (later Sir John) Habakkuk (from 1949 to 1967). Tawney retained an emeritus chair at LSE after his retirement, but, though greatly respected, he did not exercise any strong influence in a reformist direction. The phase of rapid growth proceeded in the control of what might be called a 'broad neutralist front'. It was not, of course, the conscious and cohesive entity that so political-sounding a label would suggest. But the general form and tone of economic history, as it came to be taught and researched in the expanding British universities from the 1950s to the 1970s, would certainly not have greatly appealed to those who had once seen the subject as an instrument of moral regeneration and social and economic reform.

The economic historiography which thus throve in Britain, during its rise to respectability, was of a particular type. From the careful use of primary sources, both literary and numerical, statements were built up which provided a description, partly chronological and partly functional, of a given economic activity in the past. They were placed within a framework derived from the broadest assumptions of neo-

[17] Some of the unusual circumstances attending this appointment are described in W. K. Hancock, *Country and Calling* (1954). An Australian, Hancock (later Sir Keith) was Professor of History at Birmingham University from 1934 to 1944 and in 1941 had taken charge of the official war histories. When appointed to the Oxford economic history chair he found himself having to combine his duties at the Historical Section of the War Cabinet with lecturing on British economic history since 1760 on which, as he observed, 'I had never prepared a single lecture' (p. 232). The difficult circumstances of wartime life, partly in London and partly in Oxford, proved exhausting. After visiting Australia again, in 1948, he resigned the Oxford chair.

classical economics. Profit-maximizing entrepreneurs reaped economies by introducing new techniques; scarce resources were given historical embodiments and their couplings in pursuit of given ends duly described; the constituents, structure, and movement of demand, at home and overseas, were examined and, whenever sources allowed, measured. Ashton's reaction (itself derived from Unwin) against Cunningham's concern with state policy, and, indeed, against the whole German historicist emphasis upon *Staatsbildung*, had widespread influence and ensured that past economic events were examined almost as though they existed in a vacuum. The equivalent of Acton's famous dictum that historians should study problems in preference to periods was that economic historians should study processes rather than totalities.[18] Those processes were economic sequences of apparent cause and effect, operating over periods of time chosen by reference to economic criteria. They were emphatically not stages of economic growth, be they Smithian, German historicist, Marxist, or non-Marxist. The refutation of, or at any rate detachment from, theoretical constructions claiming to explain 'the rise of capitalism', or the like, was an essential ingredient of a neutralist approach which was pragmatic, non-theoretical (save in its limited use of broadly Marshallian categories), and commonsensical. Although Ashton was its prime exponent in economic history, the general position gained philosophical support from a very different LSE luminary in the post-war years, Karl Popper, whose *The Open Society and its Enemies* (1945) and *The Poverty of Historicism* (1957) provided powerful arguments against theories of this sort.

The chosen sequences for research comprised such phenomena as the rise or decline of a specific industry, changes in the pattern of foreign trade in a given area, the consequences for agriculture of shifts in market demand, or the provision of

---

[18] Both injunctions were made in the course of inaugural lectures: for Acton's see his *Lectures on Modern History*, p. 24; for Ashton's see 'The Relation of Economic History to Economic Theory' in Harte (ed.), *Study*, pp. 165, 170.

finance for national economic expansion. The main exception to this generally sectoral approach was, of course, the very heavy concentration on the British industrial revolution. This well-known economic process became a dominant focus of interest. This dominance imposed a fixity of concern upon curricula in schools and universities alike. It was, as suggested earlier, an ultimate legacy of Toynbee's *Lectures on the Industrial Revolution*;[19] the treatment, however, had switched from reformist to neutralist. Much of real scholarly worth was achieved by these methods. But they left the pursuit of economic history in Britain rather insular in content and certainly insulated from what was happening in the wider world of historiography and of economics.

The immediately post-war scene saw no notable change in the uneasy relationship between history and economic history in Britain. Orthodox historiography was continuing to experience the reverberations of the explosion let loose by Lewis Namier in the 1930s; many publications and much discussion generated by his ideas flowed throughout the 1950s. Where the new enthusiasm for economic history was accommodated by some increase of staff within history departments, as, for example, at Manchester, the existing isolation from economics generally continued. In London, in the later 1940s and early 1950s, the standard greeting at the University's Institute of Historical Research for anyone practising economic history, and who came from LSE, was a wary mixture of hostility and contempt: the subject was barely reputable and the institution probably subversive. It was a measure of the remarkable change to come that, in 1977, the directorship of that Institute was to be taken over by an economic historian.[20] Relations between economic history and economics, though rather more cordial, were very far from intimate. Although, for example, some economic history was taught in the Cambridge Faculty of Economics and Politics and was a compulsory paper in the

[19] See above, p. 62.
[20] Professor F. M. L. Thompson.

London economics degree, it remained everywhere marginal to the economics curriculum. That curriculum was increasingly preoccupied with the extension of neo-classical micro-economic theory and the absorption of all the ramifications of Keynesian and post-Keynesian macro-economics. The new interest in economic growth theory brought economists and economic historians a little closer together, but, as will be indicated later, the result was no sort of happy marriage.

Meanwhile, as a direct consequence of this equivocal situation of economic history in Britain, the gathering momentum of post-war enthusiasm for the subject in the universities led to the creation of many separate departments of economic history. It seemed too specialized and too different from the still primarily political interests of 'straight' historians; and economists found it irrelevant to the formulation of theory and only marginal to forecasting and policy. So the logical answer was a new department, or sometimes containment within new groupings devoted to the social sciences. In the late 1940s, when British universities were returning to something like normality after six years of war, there was no such thing as a department of economic history. LSE had the biggest commitment to the subject, with six members of its staff entirely concerned with teaching it; and it was something of a boast within the School that it had no formally demarcated departments. Expansion changed all that. Growth in numbers, administrative convenience, and the familiar process of internal empire-building brought numerous departments into being. Among them was one devoted to economic history. By the 1960s its staff had more than doubled and included three professors of the subject.

The role played by LSE and London University was important both because of Ashton's prominence in consolidating and extending the neutralist position and because of the primacy and size of its commitment. Before they became degree-awarding universities in their own right a number of the former university colleges, Leicester and Exeter, for example, took London University degrees. As they grew into fully-fledged universities and, along with existing civic universities, took on board or expanded the social sciences, the creation of numerous separate departments of economic history proceeded apace. As social history also became increasingly popular and was seen as having a peculiarly intimate, albeit imprecisely defined, link with economic matters, so some such departments embraced this additional sort of history. By the 1970s, there were some fifteen separate departments of economic (or economic and social) history in British universities. Some of them even offered separate degrees in the subject. A few of the entirely new universities, for instance, Sussex and East Anglia, eschewed the creation of such separate entities and incorporated economic history into departments or faculties devoted to the social sciences or to groupings of regional studies. Inevitably, as this whole process of expansion got under way, the pioneering role of LSE ensured that several of the new separate departments or social science faculties had a large number of either LSE graduates or former LSE lecturers on their own staffs.

There were important exceptions to this pattern. In London, University College, for example, kept out of the social science bonanza and economic history developed there within its impressively large and influential history department. Oxford and Cambridge provided, of course, the biggest exceptions. Both maintained an effective resistance to the intrusion of separate departments of economic (and/or social) history; and also, for a time at least, to the recognition of such dangerous innovations as the social sciences. The continuing advance of the subject in both institutions owed much to the influence of their respective professors and of individual dons operating within the collegiate system and faculties of history and, to a lesser extent, of economics. Yet little or nothing was done to foster any significant intellectual co-operation between the two parents and their offspring. The separateness remained. Although not enshrined in separate departments,

or even separate degrees, it persisted in separate specialization, separate examination papers, and separate questions
therein. Such arrangements did have the considerable virtue
of making it impossible to do what had become possible in
some institutions: to emerge as a specialist economic historian
without ever having read any significant amount of any other
sort of history, be it about Britain or elsewhere. On the other
hand, it still remained only too possible to emerge as a teacher
or indeed university lecturer in the subject without ever
having had any formal training whatever in economics.

This separateness has manifested itself in a variety of symptoms. Several post-war inaugural lectures have shown even
more concern than their pre-war counterparts, with the
relation between economic history and its parents or its social
science siblings. Perhaps the most revealing titular expression
of awareness of this separate identity was Professor Mathias's
contribution in 1970: 'Living with the Neighbours'.[21] A
wholly different sort of symptom could be found in bookshops
catering for the university market. Here, works on economic
history have regularly appeared as a curious appendage,
usually to economics, occasionally to history—a large appendage in the 1960s and 1970s but shrunk in the 1980s. The
divorce from history in the eyes of booksellers became evident
from the standard guide to subjects issued by IBIS (International Book Information Services). It lists under History
such variants as Diplomatic History, Social History, Demographic History, Urban History, Army History, and more
besides. But no mention there of Economic History. That is to
be found under Economics. Conversely, in some publishers'
catalogues, works on economic history will not be found under
Economics (unless, perhaps, they seem to fall within the
rubric of Economic Development) but are included under
History. For the 'real' historian, however, the separateness

---

[21] 'Living with the Neighbours: the Role of Economic History' (Oxford, 1970),
reprinted in Harte (ed.), *Study*, pp. 369–83.

has recently been nicely illustrated in Professor John Kenyon's *The History Men*.[22] Surveying British historiography from the seventeenth century to the twentieth, from Walter Raleigh to Geoffrey Elton in some three hundred pages, he finds space for just fifteen pages on 'Tawney and Social History'.[23] A good deal of this brief mention, moreover, is devoted to showing that, despite Tawney's amiable eccentricity and the 'saintliness' of his character, his findings were wrong-headed and have been refuted by Trevor-Roper, Elton, *et al*. Economic history gets no mention in his index; nor do Adam Smith or John Millar, Postan or Ashton; the *English Historical Review* is there but not the *Economic History Review*.[24] There are passing textual references to Cunningham and Clapham. For the rest, all that the recent developments in the subject merit, as a coda to the pages on Tawney, is the comment that 'the advances made in economic and social history—stripped of their hampering Marxist bias—represent a wonderful advance, which could not have been foreseen twenty or thirty years ago'.[25]

Separateness had quite another side: it also meant independence. In the context of the booming interest in the subject, this signalled a gain in prestige and morale and thus naturally seemed attractive. Separate departments, in particular, helped to underline orthodoxy and respectability. And so, in turn, they contributed to complacency and the sapping of intellectual vitality. Instead of getting the best of both worlds, as autonomy promised, they helped to create a protected industry, sheltered by comforting tariff barriers from the danger of new ideas. 'Wonderful advances' there may have been—though the triumph of the neutralists over the reformists had little to do with the liquidation of a 'Marxist bias'—but separate economic history departments have not

[22] 1983. Its subtitle: *The Historical Profession in England since the Renaissance*.
[23] *The History Men*, pp. 235–50.
[24] Though it is mentioned in the text, pp. 245–6.
[25] Ibid., p. 282.

been conspicuous founts of originality. What was achieved —and I do not wish in any way to belittle the valuable work of individual scholars—was often achieved at a high cost. For the price of independence has too often been a sterility which has encompassed both lack of interest in recent trends in the use of economic analysis in historical questions and indifference towards innovations proceeding in the wider world of historiography. Some independent departments, small and inward-looking, have sat uncomfortably between economics, on the one side, and a larger and older history department, on the other. Some bigger departments have simply grown complacent. It is not, perhaps, coincidental that, over the past two decades, more indications of originality, of receptiveness to new ideas, or of breadth of outlook, have come from those scholars who, at some time in their careers, have studied or taught outside specialized economic history departments and/ or at universities where such things do not exist.

The Economic History Society has made its own contribution to separateness and complacency. At the 1926 meeting inaugurating the Society, Clapham is reported as having warned economic historians against becoming a 'craft guild' and to have told them that they should 'keep a foot in both worlds'.[26] His advice has been inadequately heeded. The self-satisfaction and exclusivity so often characteristic of the craft guild has certainly been on view in some of the doings of the Society. Such a complaint cannot readily be laid at the door of successive editors of the *Economic History Review*, who have had some real success in securing a reflection of a range of ideas and opinions; nor, more generally, at the Society's publications policy, which has also tried to disseminate knowledge of the subject at various levels of sophistication. But the Society's annual conferences long resembled little more than festive

[26] Barker, 'Beginnings', p. 15. See also the original source of these reported remarks, *Bulletin of the Institute of Historical Research* IV (1926–7), p. 109, where it is also noted that other participants at the meeting observed that the subject should be a part of history rather than economics.

gatherings of the clan. A recipe of a minimum number of papers and a comforting absence of intellectual combat ensured due regard for the sentiments of the good Dr Pangloss. Little wonder that the Society should have celebrated its golden jubilee in 1976 with a show of nostalgia and self-congratulation, even though a little writing could already be seen on the wall. It was all rather like one of those company annual general meetings when the board of directors organizes some special festivity to celebrate the highest money profits in the firm's history but the chairman fails to point out that the yield on assets has been falling for some time.

IV

Respectability, orthodoxy, separateness, complacency: these were the internal enemies of promise. What of the seeming enemies at the gate?

Reformist economic and social history was by no means dead in the 1950s and 1960s, but it had taken on a rather different colouring. The Hammonds' books continued to sell, especially in the absence of much else in the immediate post-war years; and Tawney continued to be widely admired. Nevertheless, Hammondesque liberalism and Tawneyesque socialism, though still not without influence, had ceased to command the sort of allegiance which could readily continue to shape a new generation's approach to the economic past. Much of what that sort of reformism had once sought seemed to be in reach of achievement, either willy-nilly, through the circumstances of World War II, or deliberately, through the policy commitments of successive governments. It would, however, be wholly wrong to suppose that universal content-ment reigned over orthodox economics and neutralist econom-ic history as it moved into the ascendancy. There were some new reinforcements to the old oppositional stance.

The declining impact of Tawney's voice in the Labour party during the later 1930s, in the face of shriller and harsher voices, was paralleled by the rise of a different sort of reformist economic history. Some of it was associated with G. D. H. Cole's version of socialism. Although he wrote two popularizing books, in 1934 and in 1948, about Marxism, his version of the past did not properly employ Marxist categories of analysis.[27] This was true of the book which he wrote with Raymond Postgate, *The Common People 1746–1938*. It first appeared in 1938, went to an enlarged, updated, and partly rewritten edition in 1946, and was reprinted in 1956 and 1961. So it was well-timed for the beginning of the post-war boom in economic history. Postgate is said to have written most of it.[28] Whoever was responsible, it is entirely in the 'goodies' and 'baddies' tradition, in which ordinary people are 'stunted and maimed' by the factory system or become helpless victims of 'high finance' and 'stock-market gamblers'.[29] The tone is more vituperative than Tawney's and is certainly redolent of Cole's hatred of capitalism, which, he believed, had created 'a class structure that denied most people their full individuality'.[30] In a similar vein, but more comprehensive and more specifically Marxist in approach, were such works as A. L. Morton's *A People's History of England*, first published in 1938 and reprinted more than once for post-war readers. Here historical 'goodies' and 'baddies' are unequivocally class-based: 'it cannot be too strongly insisted that the Civil War *was* a class struggle, *was* revolutionary and *was* progressive'.[31] Similarly, Christopher Hill's numerous writings, starting with *The English Revolution 1640* (1940), were much concerned to interpret the seventeenth century in overtly Marxist terms. The greater part of this sort of writing had, in truth, little to do

---

[27] *What Marx really Meant* (1934) and *The Meaning of Marxism* (1948). On Cole's attitude to Marx in general, see L. P. Carpenter, *G. D. H. Cole: An Intellectual Biography* (Cambridge, 1973), pp. 226–8.

[28] Carpenter, *G. D. H. Cole*, p. 224.

[29] *The Common People, 1764–1946* (1961 edn.), pp. 137, 149–50, 270, 654, and *passim*.

[30] Carpenter, *G. D. H. Cole*, p. 234.

[31] A. L. Morton, *A People's History of England* (1948 edn.), p. 232.

with economic history, being largely a particular sort of deter-
minist political history with a strong Marxist or quasi-Marxist
flavour. In his *Reformation to Industrial Revolution* (1967), Hill
exhibited to the full that contempt for economics so characteristic of the reformist tradition. This book, remarkably,
appeared two years later as the second volume of the Pelican
Economic History of Britain. Containing little in the way of
economics, Marxist or non-Marxist, it marked the apotheosis
of a sort of reformist economic history which maintained the
tradition of minimum analysis and maximum indignation.[32]

Of a very different calibre was the Marxist critique of
conventional economics and neutralist economic history
pioneered in Britain by a member of the Cambridge economics faculty, Maurice Dobb. His *Political Economy and Capitalism*, which came out in 1937 and was reprinted during and
after the war, provided one of the few penetrating analyses
of conventional economics available to the generation who
were going to read the subject at that time. It took Marx's
economic arguments seriously and was a long way from tub-
thumping. So, too, was his only foray into economic history,
Studies in the Development of Capitalism (1946). A product not of
research in original sources but of wide reading in secondary
material, it was highly influential in stimulating some to think
critically of the emergent neutralist orthodoxy and others to
go further and embrace Marxism as a key to the understanding of the economic past. The post-war generation of
Marxist economic historians in Britain have included the
eminent medievalist R. H. Hilton and an outstanding moder-
nist, E. J. Hobsbawm. From them, in turn, as well as from
Hill's influential teaching at Oxford, have stemmed younger
scholars who have become increasingly eclectic in combining
elements of Marxian analysis with orthodox economics and
historiography. As the tide of enthusiasm for neutralist

---

[32] Along with the third volume in that Pelican Series—Eric Hobsbawm's *Industry
and Empire* (1969), a work of far superior analytical power—it also did much to
continue some popular identification of economic history with the political Left.

economic history began to turn, this Marxist and neo-Marxist strand of reformist history provided one of the counter-attractions, not least in the 1960s and 1970s as middle-class social guilt reasserted itself. Nevertheless, the Marxist strain of economic history as a whole failed to secure a central hold on the subject in Britain. No recognizable Marxist occupied a chair in the subject in the UK until 1970, when Eric Hobsbawm was appointed to a professorship of economic and social history at Birkbeck College, London.[33] The powerful strain of pragmatism, of deep suspicion of any theoretical constructions as an aid to understanding, which was true of all forms of British historiography, was certainly one of the reasons for this failure. Just as entrenched empiricism had severely limited the use of Marshallian economics by Clapham, and also prevented any flights of theoretical fancy by Ashton and his pragmatic neutralist followers, so most of even the later and apparently radical reformists did little more than make Marxist noises. It was easy enough to offer genera-lized assertions about the transition from feudalism to capital-ism, about exploitation, oppression, and class-conflict. It was quite another matter to try to interpret original documentary sources with the aid of what was, like that part of Smith's own view of the past which orthodox British economics had conve-niently forgotten, a stage-theory of economic growth as well as a particular model of the relationship between capital and labour as a source of value.

And there was, of course, a wholly different reason: the identification of Marxism with the Soviet Union. In the 1930s, middle-class intellectuals, London- and Oxbridge-based, could vicariously identify themselves with the plight of the unemployed and the fight against Nazism in Germany, Fascism in Italy, and Franco in Spain. The visions of advance

---

[33] Hobsbawm himself is almost certainly correct in observing that Dobb's official career suffered from his long association with Marxism and the Communist Party —E. J. Hobsbawm, 'Maurice Dobb' in C. H. Feinstein (ed.), *Socialism, Capitalism and Economic Growth: Essays Presented to Maurice Dobb* (Cambridge, 1967), p. 8.

held out by the Left Book Club, the political satires purveyed at Unity Theatre, the ticket to radicalism offered by membership of the Communist Party: all could be enjoyed without looking too hard at what was going on in the USSR and be sustained, at least temporarily, by alliance in war. It was much more difficult to swallow successively the Stalin–Ribbentrop pact, the advance of the Russian moloch into eastern and central Europe, the Orwellian revelations of a totalitarian regime which proudly identified itself with the name of Marx, and, above all, the crushing of the Hungarian rising in 1956.

In 1952 there appeared a new journal, *Past and Present*, which bore the subtitle *A Journal of Scientific History*. Although it did not announce its orientation in specific terms, it remained reasonably clear that 'scientific' meant Marxist. In December 1958, however, its fourteenth issue contained a note announcing a widening of the editorial board and the statement that the journal was 'not a vehicle for the expression of any single philosophical approach'.[34] A discreet change of subtitle to *A Journal of Historical Studies* marked the next issue, in April 1959. From that time, *Past and Present* has gone from strength to strength, increasing its size and widening alike its circulation and its subject-matter. It has done more than simply shed or modify its overtly Marxist image. It has become a journal concerned not merely or largely with economic history or the economic interpretation of history, but with what has generally and vaguely come to be called social history. Statistics and graphs rarely encumber its pages; the algebra of economic formulae, never. Increasingly, the budding young historian in Britain, faced with the often rather unexciting offerings typically to be found in the pages of the *Economic History Review*, has found it hard to resist the colourful diversity of *Past and Present* articles, covering as they do an immense variety of seductive historical topics, ranging from

---

[34] *Past and Present* 14, p. 93.

witchcraft, crises, and musical taste to menstruation, rituals, and political élites. Far more effectively than Marxist historiography, social history has signalled another and different challenge to narrow, neutralist economic history.

'Social History' had no entry in the *Encyclopaedia of the Social Sciences* published in the USA in 1931. In its 1968 successor, also American, the *International Encyclopaedia of the Social Sciences*, this omission was rectified. Although the relevant section includes a discussion of what the author calls 'unschematic social history' there is no mention of the book which, in Britain during the post-war decades, provided the supreme example of that genre: G. M. Trevelyan's *English Social History*. Published first in America in 1942, its publication in Britain was delayed, because of wartime paper shortage, until 1944. It promptly became a best-seller, was reprinted several times, and achieved transmutation into both paperback and multi-volume illustrated versions. To the general British reading public it *was* social history. To the academic professional it was the apotheosis of Whig history in general and of a particular variety defined by its author as 'the history of a people with the politics left out'.[35] Trevelyan saw it as telling of 'six whole centuries of the variegated and wonderful life of England', from the making of a nation in Chaucer's day to the 'carefree Victorians'.[36] Nostalgic, chauvinistic, and snobbish, it offers, as Kenyon has rightly observed, 'a striking example of the way in which popular taste diverges so often from the academic, and ignores social trends'.[37] Certainly it became one of the prime objects of contempt for the 'scientific' social historians; and certainly it is very 'unschematic'. In the present context, however, it is worth noting that it bore a dedication, 'To the memory of Eileen Power, economic and social historian'; and that to his much-quoted definition, about history with the politics left out, Trevelyan added that

[35] G. M. Trevelyan, *English Social History* (2nd edn., 1946), p. vii.
[36] Ibid., pp. viii, 584.
[37] Kenyon, *History Men*, p. 234.

the social scene grows out of economic conditions, to much the same extent that political events in their turn grow out of social conditions. Without social history, economic history is barren and political history is unintelligible.[38]

Whether the sort of social history that Trevelyan wrote was ever likely to make economic history fertile or political history intelligible is at best questionable. And it seems likely that the Eileen Power of the dedication was more the author of *Medieval People* than the advocate of a 'genuine scientific method of abstraction and comparison' speaking in her inaugural lecture.[39] More important is the implicit, if vaguely specified, determinism of Trevelyan's dicta. Perhaps he did not fully appreciate their implications. But they certainly gave a popular confirmation to the idea, growing stronger in some academic quarters and certainly to be underlined in the earlier years of *Past and Present*, that the subject-matter of social history was essentially a part of the superstructure of economic life. This had the advantage, moreover, of offering scope for the pursuit of appropriate topics without any apparent need to know any economics or to investigate the way in which an economy worked.

This sort of social history was illuminated in a most striking fashion by Edward Thompson's *The Making of the English Working Class*, which first appeared in 1963. Very much in the reformist tradition of the Hammonds, its particular mixture of Marx and Cobbett issued a clarion call of intent.

I am seeking to rescue the poor stockinger, the Luddite cropper, the 'obsolete' hand-loom weaver, the 'utopian' artisan, and even the deluded follower of Joanna Southcott, from the enormous condescension of posterity.[40]

Vigorously and passionately written, it rapidly scored a hit amongst the more rebellious sections of the young, disenchanted with or bored by the orthodoxy of neutralist economic history. It also struck a more general responsive note in the

[38] *English Social History*, p. vii.
[39] See above, p. 90.
[40] E. P. Thompson, *The Making of the English Working Class* (1963), p. 12.

later 1960s and 1970s, as middle-class social guilt reasserted itself along with various other forms of contemporary *Angst*.

Orthodox British neutralists could readily distance themselves from this sort of social history: it carried a familiar reformist message. Nor did they show much enthusiasm for a very different venture, the incursion of American-style sociology into economic history, as represented by Neil Smelser's *Social Change in the Industrial Revolution* (1959). The onward march of social history continued, however, collecting numerous specialisms and starting new journals the while. In 1967 came two new chairs—for M. W. Flinn at Edinburgh and H. J. Perkin at Lancaster—devoted simply to social history, *tout court*.[41] Their views of the past, for example Perkin's *Origins of Modern English Society 1780–1880*, both fitted in far more readily than Thompson's with neutralist economic history. The same could not be said for some of the multiplying diversities represented in *Past and Present* or coming in from overseas. 'Social history' rapidly became a meaningless catchall term, embracing a range which included labour history and demographic history, psycho-history, family history, and women's history, not to speak of the history of magic and *mentalités*, of crowds and sports and crime, of literacy, or of children. Such specialisms as business history and agricultural history had already spawned their own journals before a flurry of new periodicals in the 1960s and 1970s signalled the new enlightenment. Most started in the USA: e.g. the *Journal of Social History* in 1967, the *Journal of Family History* in 1972, the *Journal of Psycho-History* in 1976. In Britain, *Social History* came along in 1976 to join *Past and Present*. In the same year *History Workshop* also started up, maintaining the reformist-Marxist stream and announcing it with an unequivocal subtitle, *A Journal of Socialist and Feminist Historians*. (Incidentally, the term 'workshop' to describe a seminar or similar gathering became popular at about this time, carrying as it evidently did

[41] R. H. Hilton had become Professor of Medieval Social History at Birmingham in 1963.

an aura, however phoney, of earnest manual endeavour, thereby distinguishing it from 'élitist' intellectualism.) The multiplication of specialities had proceeded so far in the USA that, already, in 1970, a *Journal of Interdisciplinary History* was thought to be necessary. Its launching was indeed a notable testimony to the current state of historiography. Its very title testifies both to the narrowness of what had once been the conventional conception of history and to the catholicity which was being achieved. Ideally, the notion of 'interdisciplinary history' should be tautological: it is the very profusion of new areas and new methods which has made it seem desirable, even necessary.

Although America was the source of many of these new enthusiasms, the most pervasive influence on the study of the subject outside Britain has been that emanating from the French *Annales* school. The deliberate act of opposition against French orthodoxy, against *l'histoire événementielle*, by Marc Bloch and Lucien Febvre, symbolized by their founding of *Annales* in 1929, sent out ripples far and wide. In Britain they did not much dent the bastions of neutralist orthodoxy. The message was an advocacy of *l'histoire totale*. Its reality, however, as transmitted first by François Simiand and later by Fernand Braudel, looked rather like a Gallic version of Marxist determinism, despite protestations to the contrary, latched on to some elements familiar from the writings of the reformists. Here is Tawney in 1932:

The only adequate history is *l'histoire intégrale*, and the limitations of specialisms can be overcome only by a treatment which does justice at once to the economic foundations, the political superstructure and the dynamic of ideas.[42]

And here is Le Roy Ladurie, some forty years later:

I have endeavoured in the present book to observe, at various levels, the long-term movements of an economy and of a society—base and superstructure, material life and cultural life, sociological evolution and collective psychology.[43]

[42] 'The Study of Economic History' in Harte (ed.), p. 106.
[43] E. Le Roy Ladurie, *The Peasants of Languedoc* (Illinois, 1976; translated by John Day from the French paperback edn. of *Les paysans de Languedoc*, Paris, 1969), p. 289.

Perhaps they were both in their different ways talking about those more important and 'better things' that Clapham had envisaged being carried by the economic foundations. Some equivalencies proposed in 1972, by an English adherent of the *Annales* school, had the effect of emphasizing this implied economic reductionism as a common characteristic. Dr Peter Burke suggested that 'our Febvre' was Tawney; our *Annales* is *Past and Present*; and that 'our Chaunu or Goubert or Le Roy Ladurie is Eric Hobsbawm, Lawrence Stone or Edward Thompson'. Maybe. In any event, Burke was certainly right to add that in practice English historians took 'much less interest in the long-term and in total history than the French'.[44]

The work of the school as a whole did not travel rapidly across the barrier of language and over the walls of British empiricism. Although Marc Bloch's investigations became known to English economic historians, thanks largely to Postan's advocacy, his approach was much less rhetorical and theoretic than that of some of his colleagues. His major works were not, however, translated until the 1960s. Braudel's celebrated *La Méditerranée et la Monde Méditerranéen à L'Époque de Philippe II*—which has a fair claim to being the most influential work of history since World War II—did not appear in English until 1972, though originally published in 1949. The less than enthusiastic British reception of the *Annales* school was due in part to the latter's dogmatic insistence upon a mechanistic analysis, conducted either according to Simiand's breaking up of the past into 'A-phases' and 'B-phases', based on price movements, or in terms of *structure, conjuncture*, and *la longue durée*; and in part to the overblown rhetoric of Braudel's style and his tendency to speak of 'les Anglo-Saxons' in much the same fashion as did General de Gaulle.

---

[44] P. Burke (ed.), *Economy and Society in Early Modern Europe. Essays from Annales* (1972), p. 9. For a more sceptical and realistic view of the *Annales* phenomenon, see Bernard Bailyn's entertaining review article on T. Stoianovich, *French Historical Method. The Annales Paradigm* in *Journal of Economic History* xxxvii (1977), pp. 1028–34.

IV

All these challenges to neutralist orthodoxy came from a changing outer world of historians, demographers, sociologists, feminists, *Annalistes, et al.* What, meanwhile, had that other world of economics to offer?

During the immediate post-war decades, the appearance of a new international economic phenomenon generated for economists a new set of practical problems, gave a powerful impetus to a hitherto neglected area of theorizing, stimulated publications, and, incidentally, offered some lucrative jobs. The problems were those which followed upon the break-up of colonial empires in Africa and Asia and the creation of numerous new national territories which were seen to be economically 'underdeveloped'. The term 'economic development', hitherto virtually unknown, became a commonplace; and 'development economics' emerged as a new branch of theory.

Economic development sounded as though it bore some relationship to economic history; possibly, indeed, by dint of the extra syllables, occupying some indefinably more impressive position. In reality, it turned out that most economists concerned with economic development largely ignored economic history; and, conversely, few economic historians found development economics helpful or congenial. According to one American economist, looking retrospectively from the vantage point of the 1980s at the growth-theories, model-building, and empirical enquiries of the 1950s, 'the field of economic history was to be revitalized from the perspective of development'.[45] Economic history got its boost but, in Britain at any rate, 'the perspective of development' soon began to lose whatever appeal it may have had for most economic historians, the more the relevant theory was spelled out. That this should have been so was partly due to the pervasive difficulty—not confined to this particular area of economics,

[45] Gerald M. Meier in Gerald M. Meier and Dudley Seers (eds.), *Pioneers in Development* (Oxford, 1984), p. 19.

but here illustrative of a more general obstacle—of putting historical flesh upon economic models. Growth models were notoriously absent in the corpus of neo-classical economics; and the adaptation of Keynesian concepts to this problem, in the shape of the Harrod-Domar equation, aroused little enthusiasm among British economic historians (even if they knew what it was). The regard for the particular and for evidence, which the historian treasures, did not look kindly upon hypotheses considered as potentially applicable to anywhere from West Africa to the Phillipines.[46] Marx's growth-model, though long available, did not, for obvious reasons, commend itself to Western economists or historians as a solvent for these new problems—though Maurice Dobb provided some perceptive and characteristically elegant critical contributions in *An Essay on Economic Growth and Planning* (1960).

The only major growth-model contributed by a professor of economic history, that of the American, W. W. Rostow, tended, eventually, to reinforce the disenchantment. Adumbrated in *The Process of Economic Growth* (1951) and popularized in *The Stages of Economic Growth* (1960), complete with the subtitle of *A Non-Communist Manifesto*, Rostow's concept of a 'take-off into self-sustained growth', leading to an age of 'high mass-consumption', ran foul of neutralist economic historians and also of a good many economists. It did so in sundry ways which need not be specified here.[47] It may, however, be worth noting that its deterministic character had been foreshadowed in his earlier study, *British Economy of the Nineteenth Century* (1948), in the course of which the significant passage from Trevelyan's *Social History*, cited above, was approvingly quoted as indicative of his own approach.[48] The whole theory,

[46] See, for example, K. E. Berrill's review article on W. A. Lewis, *Theory of Economic Growth* (1955) in *Econ. Hist. Rev.* 2nd Ser. IX (1956), pp. 359–63.

[47] For some examples see A. K. Cairncross, 'The Stages of Economic Growth', *Econ. Hist. Rev.* 2nd Ser. XIII (1961), pp. 450–8; W. W. Rostow (ed.), *The Economics of Take-off into Sustained Growth* (1963); and B. E. Supple, 'Revisiting Rostow', *Econ. Hist. Rev.* 2nd Ser. XXXVII (1984), pp. 107–14.

[48] W. W. Rostow, *British Economy of the Nineteenth Century* (Oxford, 1948), pp. 134–5. For the Trevelyan passage see above, p. 116.

based on the alleged experience of Britain and extended to numerous other countries, had the merit of helping to encourage the collection of many new historical statistics and the construction of estimates of national incomes and outputs. In Britain, the most important of these undertakings—though not directly attributable to Rostovian stimulation—was the pioneering contribution by P. Deane and W. A. Cole, *British Economic Growth 1688–1959* (1962). For Rostow's model, however, there would today probably be general agreement with a recent verdict dismissing it as 'a grand if empty theory with the merit . . . of stimulating controversy'.[49]

A different sort of challenge to British economic history orthodoxy also travelled across the Atlantic, though it did not have any significant impact until the later 1960s. Much has been written about the nature of 'cliometrics' or the 'new economic history'.[50] But before looking at British reactions thereto, it may be desirable to sketch certain basic features of this sort of history.

First, it is not one single homogenous, monolithic method, but embraces more than one technique for analysing the past. Second, the main common feature of these techniques is the devising of explicit models specifying relationships amongst such variables as income, output, prices, exports, investment, etc.; the models are normally expressed in algebraic form. Third, the models are then tested against observed 'reality' in the shape of quantified data, for example, time-series of the relevant variables or proxies thereof. From the appropriate calculations, statements can then be made of the probability that the model does indeed 'predict' and, therefore, 'explain' the observed historical relationship of the variables. To this

---

[49] D. N. McCloskey in Roderick Floud and Donald McCloskey (eds.), *The Economic History of Britain since 1700* (2 vols., Cambridge, 1981), I, p. 105.

[50] The best general discussions and guides thereto are necessarily American, e.g. R. L. Andreano (ed.), *The New Economic History: Recent Papers on Methodology* (New York, 1970); R. D. McClelland, *Causal Explanation and Model Building in History, Economics and the New Economic History* (New York, 1975) which has a very full bibliography; and, more briefly, R. W. Fogel and G. R. Elton, *Which Road to the Past?* (New Haven, 1983).

necessarily bare statement of common elements it should be added that practice ranges from, say, simple hypotheses about the correlation of two time-series to more sophisticated econometric models, involving several variables; and that sometimes the models involve explicit counterfactual hypotheses. All such models, however, have certain vitally important features, which identify both their strength and their limitations. First, they depend for their practical value upon quantification. They are, therefore, mainly suitable for use with questions involving large numbers, the levels of which lie outside the conscious control of single individuals, for example, prices determined in a free market or the size and movements of a national population. Second, they are built upon various sets of assumptions about aggregate human behaviour (for example, that businessmen seek continuously to maximize short-term profits to the exclusion of other aims) and about prevailing economic relationships (for example, that perfect competition prevails, that costs are constant, or that demand functions are linear).

So much, in broadest outline, for the character of the new economic history. What of its reception in Britain? As a logical extension of the neutralist position, it might have been expected to generate a friendly response. In reality, however, it got a fairly dusty answer. It did not provoke the fierce hostility which was the answer of many orthodox historians in the USA, to the extent that, as was claimed in 1975, 'two warring camps confront each other with distrust, occasional hostility, and a minimum of communication'.[51] There, however, the onslaughts of the cliometricians had been directed against venerable and emotive targets of American historical enquiry, such as the profitability or otherwise of southern plantation slavery. Moreover, as economic history was mainly taught in economics departments in the USA, the onslaughts had been seen by historians there as coming from intrusive, upstart number-crunchers. By the time that the new economic

[51] McClelland, *Causal Explanation*, p. 243.

history had crossed the Atlantic its impact had been dulled; and it had not touched any sacred cows of British historiography. So 'straight' historians in Britain largely ignored it; and most economic · historians remained critical or, at best, unenthusiastic.

The reformists were more or less inevitable enemies of cliometrics, in so far as the new economic historians used the techniques of conventional economics, were not evidently propelled by middle-class social guilt, and seemed little disposed to deploy their findings on the economic past in the cause of reforming the industrial present. The neutralists took up an essentially sceptical stand. Their reasons were by no means all trivial. The new understanding seemed too often to be irrelevant, inappropriate, or inapplicable to many questions in European history; or to be built upon unrealistic assumptions (not always made explicit) of a perfectly competitive world of profit-maximizers and marginal adjusters. Specimens of cliometric procedure revealed a too ample flood of regression analyses, run on any old collection of data without heed of historical context, yet purporting to offer scientific truth. High ingenuity was too readily lavished upon topics of limited scope or was productive of answers of limited applicability. Endless bickering over the minutiae of model-specification threatened to constitute a new branch of antiquarianism. To scepticism was added resentment, in reaction to some arrogant trumpeting by the new men and their camp followers, replete with contemptuous sneers about 'old' (= old-fashioned) economic history. In the light of more recent self-criticism, of the adoption of a more moderate tone, and of a growing awareness, even amongst the faithful, that cliometrics does not provide the only route to the economic past, it might reasonably seem that British indifference or aversion was more than a little justified.

Nevertheless, such retrospective cheer about a band-wagon which may have ceased to roll as rapidly as it once did should not be allowed to screen the fact that its reception by British economic historians showed rather more complacency and conservatism than is good for any intellectual activity. That this was so owed something to the existence of those separate economic history departments and something to an older weakness in the British educational structure.

Almost certainly, only a very few economic historians, educated in Britain and teaching and publishing in their subject in the 1950s and 1960s, would have passed any university-level course in statistics or be capable of more than the most elementary manipulation of quantitative data; still fewer would have read and be competent to use a book such as R. G. D. Allen's *Mathematical Analysis for Economists*, which had been in print since 1938. Amongst those who had taken an economics degree, a majority would have quitted the formal study of economics to specialize in economic history just at the point when the former demanded more statistical or mathematical understanding. Hardly any British undergraduates of the same period would have combined history and mathematics in their qualifications for entry to university; indeed, at most schools, unusual ingenuity was required to combine these subjects at A level. The deep-seated habit of early specialization in schools ensured, *inter alia*, that generations of putative historians in Britain could never even imagine that algebra might be a useful tool to help unlock any doors of the past. Many found even the simplest statistical treatment of historical data incomprehensible and/or repellant. In 1959 the Crowther Report, *15 to 18*, in tackling the problem of 'literacy' and 'numeracy' observed pertinently: 'When we say that a historian or a linguist is "innumerate" we mean that he cannot even begin to understand what scientists and mathematicians are talking about'. It went on to add that the majority of schools ignored the problem and made no provision for solving it.[52]

Consequently, as economic history boomed in post-war Britain, it drew in many people who, for good reasons or bad,

[52] *15 to 18: Report of the Central Advisory Council for Education (England)* (HMSO, 1959), vol. I, pp. 270, 277.

were either turning their backs upon 'numeracy' or had never acquired it. Corralled within the comforting walls of economic history departments, the general tenor of their response to this particular challenge was to look with a mixture of critical distaste and at least partial incomprehension at the cliometric breakers coming in on the Atlantic tide. There were, as already mentioned, good reasons for some of the criticism. But one of the results of this whole sequence of events was certainly to add to the separateness of economic history in Britain.

By the 1960s and 1970s, most orthodox British historians, devoting their time to the conventional subjects of their calling—from medieval charters to twentieth-century diplomacy—would have been wholly incapable of following the arguments being deployed in some of the learned articles, and even a few of the books, in economic history. This would have been especially true of the *Journal of Economic History* and of certain books published in the USA, and rather less true of the *Economic History Review*, though even the British journal had by this time an increasing reflection of the new trends in the subject. So 'straight' historians left the task of comprehension to their colleagues in economic history. Many of them, however, were wholly or partially in the same boat. Whereas their counterparts in the USA were, in general, already economists in economics departments, in Britain only a very small proportion of economic historians were so placed and had the requisite technical knowledge. The majority, in their separate departments, thus found themselves further distanced from both historians and economists, despite the fact that the latest trends were coming from the latter direction. Some, of course, especially of a younger generation and whatever their undergraduate origins, took the trouble to learn the new language and became a vanguard of new economic historians in Britain. Many others pursued their older ways, wrapping up in the cloaks either of neutralist orthodoxy or of reformist indignation, and letting new ideas of whatever origin pass them by.

VI

In these various ways, the study of economic history in Britain, once a formidable component of the opposition to conventional political economy, as well as to conventional historiography, was variously supported and traduced, was rocketed upwards and then allowed to succumb to the perils of respectability. Reformist economic history of the older sort was, at least in part, replaced by quasi-, neo-, or pseudo-Marxist social history. The neutralist strain, having attained the status of an orthodoxy of its own, became separated and sterilized, too often bereft of much intellectual excitement. At a lower level in the educational hierarchy, it came to be seen as a soft-option haven for the worthy but unadventurous. In reality, of course, it is the very opposite, demanding a wider range of skills and understanding than conventional historiography. Fortunately, there are signs that a younger generation has recently been coming to terms with the claims of statistical and mathematical manipulation, rejecting the more dogmatic and fatuous pretensions, and taking on board the real contributions it has to make. Much of what is intellectually interesting and path-breaking is now proceeding on the edges of economic history, on its borderland with other sorts of history —social, demographic, political, technological, to give but some examples—or where the economic is seen as merely a part, not necessarily either the most fundamental or the most important, of a larger historical whole.

7

The Future of the Economic Past

... we are here verging on the high theme of economic progress; and here therefore it is especially needful to remember that economic problems are imperfectly presented when they are treated as problems of static equilibrium, and not of organic growth. For though the statical treatment alone can give us definiteness and precision of thought, and is therefore a necessary introduction to a more philosophic treatment of society as an organism; it is yet only an introduction.

Alfred Marshall, *Principles of Economics* (1920)[1]

I

FOR all his achievement in clearing the way to 'definiteness and precision of thought' among English-speaking economic historians, Marshall's hope for a 'more philosophical treatment of society as an organism' has certainly not been fulfilled. In its journey from the 'philosophical history' of Smith and Millar to the 'new economic history' of today, what the subject has gained in the exact specification of economic problems it has lost in increased constriction and separateness from the rest of history.

Much of the modern use of economic theory in history rests essentially upon some variant of short-period, neo-classical analysis.[2] The assumptions embodied in the parameters of the

[1] *Principles* (8th edn.), p. 461. This cautionary passage does not appear in the first edn.

[2] This remains true despite critical comments by econometric historians from the later 1960s onwards. See, e.g., Meghnad Desai, 'Some Issues in Econometric History', *Econ. Hist. Rev.* 2nd Ser. xxi (1968), pp. 1–16, and for a much more recent criticism, Stephen Nicholas, 'Total Factor Productivity and the Revision of Post-1870 British Economic History', *Econ. Hist. Rev.* 2nd Ser. xxxv (1982), pp. 83–98.

model can presume to some degree of realism because of the very limitations of time and place. As similar techniques are extended to longer periods of the past, so they have to rest less on testable economic theory and more upon either simple statistical manipulation or, in the absence of such data, upon broad theoretic abstractions for which supporting evidence is at best ambiguous. Marshall was aware of the inappropriateness of his analytical tool-kit for dealing with the larger and longer questions of history. His latter-day successors seem more optimistic and less cautious. To some of the new breed, economic history is only marginally a particular branch of history; it is primarily a branch of economics, itself a social science of a sort particularly suited to the use of mathematical techniques. If one of the prime aims of economics is to 'find the underlying regularities in the interaction of economic variables and, wherever possible, to formulate these regularities in the language of mathematics',[3] then economic history as a branch of economics correspondingly seeks the same end for past economies. Concerned with the performance of economies in the past, it distinguishes itself from 'general historical inquiry' by 'its appeal to a systematic body of theory as a source of generalization and by the equally systematic use of quantitative methods of organizing evidence'.[4] If economic history is a branch of economics, and economics a form of science, and science 'implies the objectives of explanation, prediction, and control',[5] then economic historians of this 'scientific' sort can be seen as potential contributors to the making of economic policy; and, moreover, not just by dint of being professional historians with learned views on the past but by reason of their 'scientific' analysis of data from the past.

Such 'scientific' economic history is at its most valid and

[3] McClelland, *Causal Explanation*, p. 219.
[4] Douglass C. North, 'Economic History' in *International Encyclopaedia of the Social Sciences* vol. 6 (1968), p 468.
[5] McClelland, *Causal Explanation*, p. 107.

useful when it is tackling just those types of issues for which Marshallian economics was also best fitted; with, also, the additional advantage of modern and more sophisticated techniques of estimation and calculation. Carefully specified and delimited questions about, for example, the effects of the imposition of tariffs in the 1930s, the consequences of overseas lending in the decade before World War I, or the role of capital accumulation during the industrial revolution can be answered with a higher probability of truth than was attainable by the cruder methods of the past. That it remains probability and not certainty, however, needs as much stress as should properly be given to an orthodox historian's findings about, say, the consequences of Walpole's methods of political management or of the general election of 1931. The uncertainties arise largely from the assumptions underlying the parameters of the model, often cultural, social, or political, and incapable of quantification or precise estimation.

The longer the period and the wider the area covered, the greater the uncertainty and the more dubious such techniques become. Comparison of two very different types of such exercises reveals something of the difficulties.

Matthews, Feinstein, and Odling-Smee, *British Economic Growth 1856–1973* is an analysis, cast in terms of Keynesian ideas plus national accounting techniques, of the main aggregate economic variables of one definable political entity over some 120 years.[6] The authors' chosen 'growth-accounting' method measures the statistical entity called 'total factor productivity', the ratio resulting from analysing the contribution of total inputs to total outputs, the remuneration of those contributions being assumed to be proportionate to their marginal products. If there is growth in total factor productivity, then it must arise from sources outside the increases in the measured inputs. So, total factor productivity is also, and

[6] R. C. O. Matthews, C. H. Feinstein, and J. C. Odling-Smee, *British Economic Growth 1856–1973* (Oxford, 1982).

very revealingly, sometimes called 'the residual'. This un-explained residual can thus cover anything not measured by this procedure, for example, increasing returns to scale, technical advance, removal of restrictive practices by trade unions, improvements in management, changes in government policy or international agreements. In short, all manner of influences—demographic, technological, institutional, political, social, or cultural—'commonly regarded as outside the scope of economics or at best on its fringe'[7] are treated as 'exogenous', meaning they are left out of this piece of history. From the vantage point of economic history seen as past economics, this is a wholly reasonable statement to make. Indeed, it is to the credit of the authors of this important piece of analysis that they present the assumptions and limitations in so explicit a fashion. From the viewpoint of the historian, however, it cannot but seem to omit not merely a variety of issues and influences which were probably important but to ignore all the more fascinating, because imponderable, matters of human behaviour. If this is the price of economic precision, some will undoubtedly ask whether it is worth paying.

In contrast to this treatment of these matters as exogenous, a very different model of economic growth, developed by Douglass North, treats just such matters as endogenous, as capable of being incorporated within a comprehensive theory of economic motivation. In 1971 he and Lance Davis adumbrated a 'theory of institutional change' as an explanation of American economic growth.[8] Then in 1973, jointly with R. P. Thomas, he extended the notion to offer a theoretical explanation of the rise of western Europe from 900 to 1700.[9] It explained change in terms of factor costs and property rights. Institutional change—new technologies in agriculture or new

---

[7] Ibid., pp. 15–19.
[8] Lance E. Davis and D. C. North, *Institutional Change and American Economic Growth* (Cambridge, 1971).
[9] D. C. North and R. P. Thomas, *The Rise of the Western World* (Cambridge, 1973).

organizations, such as the manor or banks—happened only when private returns thereon were expected to exceed their costs, including transaction costs. As expectations of private returns equalling social returns grew, so governments took over the protection and enforcement of property rights. All forms of invention and innovation were thus presented as economically induced by shifts in the availability and cost of factors. Eight years later, North elaborated and lengthened the theory still further by offering it as an explanation of economic change from neolithic times to the present day.[10] The neo-classical model of marginal adjustment in pursuit of individual utility maximization was here modified by the theory of institutional change, embracing both the state and property rights and also a 'theory of ideology'. All institutions were represented as, in effect, constraints limiting individual maximization and, thereby, making human organization possible. So in the end, economic history is 'conceived as a theory of the evolution of constraints'. It should, thus, not only explain past economic performance but also 'provide the modern social scientist with the evolving contextual framework within which to explain the current performance of politico-economic systems'.[11]

These two very different sorts of exercises in the explanation of economic change, one British and one American, illustrate vividly the dilemma of economic history as past economics. In the one, impressive quantitative precision is obtained with empirical data by dint of leaving out all institutional influences. In the other, by a massive sweep of imaginative abstraction, all such influences are brought within the fold by making them ultimately economic in origin. Both have at their base the potent assumptions of neo-classical marginal maximization theory. One version keeps them severely limited to what are conventionally regarded as economic phenomena;

[10] D. C. North, *Structure and Change in Economic History* (New York, 1981).
[11] Ibid., p. 209.

the other lets them run loose through all manner of behaviour by individuals and governments.

Those for whom the study of the economic past is less a branch of economics than simply one part of the totality of historical enquiry are likely to react rather differently to each of these two exercises. Bold abstractions over 10,000 years of human history, based on the primacy of economic motives, are unlikely to commend themselves to historians grappling with the complex factual evidence of the diverse source materials of everyday life. They may seem to add up to another and too ambitious a version of Smith's stage-theory, powered by that 'uniform, constant and uninterrupted effort' at self-betterment; or, to some, seem less convincing than the alternative Marxian engine of class conflict. It might even merely induce wonder about the practical use of a highly imaginative piece of intellectual fun. Conversely, an historian's reactions to the other account, of 120 years of economic growth in one country, would more likely resemble those attending the receipt of an expert report. Its empirical and statistical basis would be cheering (to those who understood it) though its unconcealed exclusion of the non-economic and non-measurable would cause warning bells to ring. Its potential role as an aid to future policy might well clash with the historian's reluctance to see himself in the role of a prophet.

Ultimately, both might seem rather too reminiscent of the optimistic rationalism of the Enlightenment. Economics, having its roots in that soil, has never lost the appropriate bloom. As Kenneth Arrow has remarked, 'an economist by training thinks of himself as the guardian of rationality, the ascriber of rationality to others, and the prescriber of rationality to the social world'.[12] But an historian, by training and by confrontation with the records of the past, knows that they reveal a world in which rationality was tossed hither and thither by the winds of religious bigotry, patriotic zeal, political

[12] Kenneth J. Arrow, *The Limits of Organization* (New York, 1974), p. 16.

ambition, or mere uncertainty; in which profit-maximizing was tempered by idealism, snobbery, lust, laziness, ritualism, or mere blundering incompetence; and in which the interplay of myth, ignorance, hysteria, and charismatic leadership has often proved as potent as the rational mind in shaping the course of events. The economist believes in rationality; the historian in scepticism. The one seeks to explain, predict, advise, control; the other has as his task to make some sense of the past and communicate it to others, thus helping to generate a new set of myths for the future. In a history-conscious society, such as ours, those myths help to sustain our consciousness of reality, our sense of belonging to a continuous tradition, ever changing, but also surviving.

II

From its present somewhat unsatisfactory situation, the study of economic history in Britain could move in an increasingly quantitative direction to follow the American trail towards becoming simply a branch of economics. It would seem a logical move for the neutralists, imparting to the subject greater intellectual rigour, making it apparently more 'scientific', and thereby strengthening its claims as a guide to economic policy. The rapidly increasing familiarity with computers in both schools and universities might readily stimulate renewed interest and make such a study attractive to young enquiring minds. Furthermore, this growing familiarity could also be harnessed to the development of various simulation techniques to test models of historical economies. And it might even be supposed that economists themselves would gain by greater intercourse with a sort of historian who would talk in their own language. The practical corollary of all this would be that more economic history should be taught in economics departments or faculties; or, where separate economic history departments survive, that intellectual demands rather tougher than those now normally made should be imposed on undergraduates, in order to improve their technical equipment in economics and statistics.

Whether economists would be willing for increased resources thus to be devoted to economic history, even of this unequivocally economic sort, is, of course, quite another matter. It is over a dozen years since Sir Henry Phelps Brown told his fellow economists: 'it has been long agreed that the economist is not trained who is not numerate; but neither is he trained if he is not historiate'. The study of history, he said, should be 'an essential part of the training of the economist'.[13] The triumph of economics over political economy, of marginalism over the historical school, having relegated the economic past to a very subordinate place in the thinking of most economists, still leaves its mark today. There are some signs of change, as various institutionalist theories surface or resurface. With a few notable exceptions, however, the majority of economists probably still tend to regard the past as irrelevant, save as a service facility, a testing ground for models. Such an attitude is certainly an advance on McCulloch's use of it as a parade ground for the display of economic folly, but it suggests the likelihood of a lukewarm attitude both to the Phelps Brown recipe for the complete economist and to the successful lodgement of economic history in the curricula of economics departments.

But, supposing that could be achieved, how to avoid the distancing between economic history and the rest of history which is the obvious concomitant of steering the former into the embrace, even if hardly a passionate one, of economics departments? It seems likely that the only way in which this can be secured is by determined and sustained attempts to integrate the teaching and examining of economic history, in whichever department or faculty it is taught, with other sorts of history. In practice, this will mean that both in separate economic history departments and where the subject is taught within history or social science departments, putative economic

[13] 'The Underdevelopment of Economics', *Econ Jnl.* LXXXII (1972), pp. 8–9.

historians must learn enough economics and statistics to understand and use those necessary tools of the economist, as well as enough history to understand and use the methods of the historian. This in itself, however, will not be enough. In some measure, a limited degree of such integration already exists where, for example, economic history papers are taken within the framework of a history degree. Yet, the lecture courses, the teaching, the examination papers are nearly always separated from each other by an intellectual hygiene barrier which ensures that questions are very rarely asked about the financing of politics or the politics of finance, that social structure and cabinet government are kept in as watertight compartments as, say, industry and kingship. It is interesting to note, moreover, that continued separateness seems to be the unspoken implication of the otherwise admirable indications of mutual tolerance and understanding in Fogel and Elton's *Which Road to the past?* (1983). The roads have no evident point of convergence.

Before pursuing the implications of any attempt to break down that barrier, it is worth considering how much the barrier itself owed its existence to the efforts of the Webbs in their establishment of the very institution which has set so enduring a seal on the study of the subject in Britain. In February 1900, congratulating themselves on their success in getting LSE 'recognized as a Faculty of Economics' in the University of London, Beatrice went on to note in her diary what she saw as Sidney's particular achievement.

Best of all he has persuaded the Royal Commission to recognise economics as a science and not merely as a subject in the Arts Faculty. The preliminary studies for the economics degree will, therefore, be mathematics and biology. This divorce of economics from metaphysics and shoddy history is a great gain. ... Such history as will be taught at the School will be the history of social institutions discovered from documents, statistics and the observation of the actual structure and working of living organizations.[14]

[14] Beatrice Webb, *Our Partnership* (1948), p. 195.

Presumably, 'shoddy' history was any sort of history which did not conform to the prescribed history of social institutions—a form of history which was evidently to be pursued by the amassing of data in the best Webbian manner and without the aid of theory. Whatever the Webbs might have made of the sundry sorts of history taught at the School in its post-World War II expansion, they would certainly have been able to cheer the severity of the divorce of economics from considerations of metaphysics or history. But they would have found remarkably few students of any variety of history with a significant competence in mathematics, let alone biology. The Webbs 'divorce' has proved more potent and lasting in the everyday procedures of teaching and examining—and not only at LSE—than Eileen Power's optimistic vision in 1933 of economists, historians, and sociologists advancing in co-operative endeavour.[15]

If the gap between economic history and other sorts of history is to be narrowed, and at the same time the peculiar requirements of economic history maintained, then the goal seems most likely to be reached if the subject concerns itself, in the practical procedures of teaching and examining, with manageable historical entities. Such entities might, for example, be regions, towns, firms, or institutions, as distinct from sectors of economic activity, such as agriculture, trade, transport, or the like. This is not, of course, to suggest that sectors or processes should be ignored, but rather to advocate far more concern with entities than at present is fashionable. They open themselves up to the multi-faceted analysis of historical experience in a way that sectors do not. Far too much of British economic historiography, in what has become the orthodox neutralist tradition, has been of the latter sort; too little of the former. There are, however, some encouraging signs and reasons for hope in what has been happening in the wider analysis of entities. One of the clear successes in British

[15] See above, p. 90.

historiography over the past half-century has been the enormous improvement in the standard of local history. Aided by contemporaneous changes for the better in county archives, it has been removed from the province of the anti-quarian and turned into a flourishing area of economic, politi-cal, and social history. It has come to embrace such diverse aspects of local historical life as demography, law enforce-ment, or literacy. Integration is far from complete in its teaching and examining. But nobody can today make a serious study of, say, seventeenth-century England without heeding a growing number of county studies bearing upon power, economy, religious affiliation, population change, and the social order. The historical reconstruction of local commu-nities demands a variety of skills—economics as well as social anthropology, demography as well as politics. Few, if any, historians can hope to command them all. But the aim of integration must remain in the mind even if it is not always realized. The same applies to urban history, a variant of local history which has also come to flourish in Britain of late years. Another promising path towards integration, it has attracted scholars able and willing to combine the use of economic arguments with the study of local administration, town plan-ning, and urban architecture; or to put the historical analysis of civic ritual alongside that of wealth and occupational structure.

The study of business history offers another hopeful avenue of recovery. It also gives enlightenment of a different sort. Because its growth illustrates some typical (as well as some untypical) aspects of recent British economic historiography and its problems, it is worth considering in some detail.

The initiative which set it going on scholarly lines in Britain came not from the economic historians but from the business-men. In the 1930s, G. N. Clark had stressed the value of business records;[16] he and Ashton had given support to the

[16] In his inaugural lecture at Oxford in 1932, in Harte (ed.), *Study*, pp. 77, 79.

recently formed Council for the Preservation of Business Archives;[17] the Bank of England had commissioned a 250th anniversary history from Clapham.[18] The initiative for the first of the major academic histories of modern British business firms came, however, from Unilever, in the shape of an approach in 1947 to Clark. He had by then moved to Cambridge and he, in turn, passed the enquiry on to Charles Wilson whose *History of Unilever* established a pattern which has continued to this day.[19] Commissioning has indeed increased substantially over the past three decades; nationalized industries have joined the queue which began in the private sector. Chemicals, textiles, glass, brewing, steel, metal manufacturing, tobacco, insurance, banking, oil, electricity supply, coal mining, railways: in all these and more, business histories of high scholarly quality have appeared in response to specific commissions. The scale of production has sometimes been quite lavish. Three big firms alone have notched up eight substantial volumes between them; another is on course for a further three; and one nationalized industry's commission will generate no less than five volumes.[20] As a form of out-relief for indigent economic historians—or at any rate those who could show eligibility—it has proved always more interesting and often more lucrative than writing textbooks.

Certain features of these British business histories stand out. They draw upon the traditional methods of the historian because they focus, as they have to by their very nature, upon many questions other than the economic: matters, for instance, of power, of politics, of organization and size, of

---

[17] Subsequently transformed into what is now the Business Archives Council.

[18] J. H. Clapham, *The Bank of England. A History* (2 vols., Cambridge, 1944).

[19] Charles Wilson, *The History of Unilever* (3 vols., 1954 and 1968), see I, p. v. It is not without significance that Unilever is not simply a British firm but is Anglo-Dutch, and that both Clark and Wilson had worked on Dutch as well as English history.

[20] The three firms with eight volumes between them are Unilever, Imperial Chemical Industries, and Courtaulds; British Petroleum is due for three; and the outcome of the National Coal Board's commission will be a five-volume history of the British coal mining industry.

personality in management, as well as of technical change. They are all cast in the neutralist mould. Accordingly, they have all been largely uninformed by any explicit use of theory beyond, again, the broad framework provided by the most general concepts of neo-classical economics, though some have drawn to a limited extent on the theoretical structures built up by Edith Penrose and Alfred Chandler.[21] Broadly speaking, the general form of these works has been that of a straightforward account of investment, production, sales, entrepreneurial actions, and personalities within the firm, together with some analysis of costs, the whole contained within a chronological narrative. It is a form open to the type of attack on absence of use of economic theory and lack of meaningful generalizations about business behaviour which was common twenty or more years ago in the USA, where business history started much earlier and against a rather different historical background. And, finally, they typify both the separateness and the ambiguity of purpose so character- istic of economic history in Britain. They sit in an indeterm- inate fashion between 'usefulness' and 'scholarship'. Commissioning itself has a complex motivation. It has some affinity with competitive prestige advertising and business patronage of the arts. It depends more upon the whims of individual chairmen or directors than upon any belief that the outcome may influence policy formulation. The resulting volumes repose impressively on sundry shelves, largely unread by anyone, save other business historians. Members of the commissioning company will occasionally dip into them out of curiosity about past leaders of the firm. Few profes- sional economists have the slightest interest in them because the history of individual businesses is not seen as doing any- thing to help the theory of the firm. Business schools largely ignore them in the teaching of the nation's future managers.

[21] E. T. Penrose, *The Theory of the Growth of the Firm* (1959); Alfred D. Chandler, jun., *Strategy and Structure* (Cambridge, Mass., 1962) and *The Visible Hand* (Cambridge, Mass., 1977).

Reformist historians, and especially the Marxist variety, look suspiciously at the supposed consequences of taking capitalist money; 'straight' historians still wonder if this 'applied history' is quite proper as a form of scholarship. The normal reviewing fate of such books, outside specialist periodicals, is either to be ignored entirely or to be given to a journalist, who can be guaranteed to complain that the presence of statistics or the language of economics spoils a jolly story. It is hardly surprising that Britain has only one chair of business history and that that dates from as recently as 1983, when the country's economic decline had become so obvious as to suggest that the historical doings of British businessmen might merit further serious investigation.[22]

Business history offers hope, however, not because it can be represented as 'relevant' (a dangerous criterion) but because it presents, in an acute form, the need for the economic historian to draw upon more than economics and also to formulate his own theories for testing against empirical evidence.

It is clear that the standard set of theoretical questions and methods available in the new economic history is of very limited value when tackling the history of the firm, the most important single organizational entity of modern economic life. Given adequate data, it is, of course, possible to pose, for example, counterfactual propositions; and, given adequate competence, to bring familiar techniques of statistical analysis to bear upon them. The resulting concentrated insight, albeit more rigorously obtained, on specific decisions has necessarily to be secured, however, at the cost of abstraction from the full historical context of those decisions. The result may tell one that, on certain assumptions, it would have been more profitable for the firm to have followed one course of action rather than another. Such a conclusion, if well-grounded in

[22] Leslie Hannah was appointed as Professor of Business History in the University of London at LSE.

appropriate techniques of both history and economics, might well be of real value to a firm in helping to shape policy. But an assemblage of such findings would no more constitute a history of the business entity than an assemblage of findings about constitutional liberty would provide an adequate history of the revolution of 1688. For the general pursuit of business history, the type of theory developed by Chandler in his analysis of strategy and structure goes a long way towards the provision of an appropriate historical framework. It may well be that such neo-institutionalist theories will turn out to be more useful, not only in business history but in wider areas of economic history generally, than those currently in vogue among economic historians of the newer sort.

III

To summarize. No longer a focus of intellectual opposition to traditional history orthodoxy, and having lost the momentum imparted by its oppositional role, economic history in Britain has lost one sense of purpose and is only just beginning to find another. Its future health needs the breaking down of barriers separating history, economic history, and economics. If we know a little more today about the whole history of a village or a town, a country or a region—or, for that matter, of a war or a revolution—we are still far from the integrated history of a nation or a continent. We need more historical examination of irrational economic man in a political and social context, and rather less of rational man in a vacuum. It is as vital that the subject should be better integrated with the wider range of history as that it should draw upon economics and the other social sciences. But, to achieve that, economic historians must not wait upon economists to provide the theoretical models; they must be prepared to construct and test their own. Just as in business history it has become crucial to move outside the individual firm, to pursue 'systematic integrative work going beyond company history towards comparative business

history',[23] so in other areas there must be developed the study
of a two-way historical relationship between the economy and
the polity, between the creation and distribution of wealth and
the creation and distribution of power. Too often this last has
been left to assumption rather than subjected to analysis. The
reductionist fallacy has been allowed to sustain the notion
that, in some imprecisely specified way, actions 'reflect' price
movements or other economic indicators; that culture, like
trade, follows the flag of economic change.

These observations carry a variety of implications. They
imply, for instance, that the Economic History Society would
do well to abandon the aura of Pangloss and take a lead in
stimulating serious debate; and this also means efforts to
raise the level of teaching in schools. Happily, there are signs
that steps are being taken to this end. Faced with current
government policies which are reducing real resources in all
higher education, as well as downgrading the study of history,
the need for action is all the more pressing. They also imply
no weeping over the likely demise of small and vulnerable
separate economic history departments. The bigger and
stronger departments which survive will need to justify their
separateness. Another probable implication is that, within the
normal university structure, the subject should ideally be
taught in both history and economics departments. This may
seem wasteful or untidy but it is hard to see an easier way of
coping really adequately with the subject's inherent duality.
Whatever the departmental arrangements, however, a further
corollary is the need for co-operation, closer than has hitherto
been customary, in both history and economics; and for real
integration in both teaching and examining. The possibility of
achieving such co-operation should be greater today than
formerly. In some universities, economic and social history
has for some time been a required element in a history degree.

[23] L. Hannah, 'New Issues in British Business History', *Business History Review* LVII
(Summer, 1983), p. 166.

And so it should be. Without some understanding of the historical experience of economic life as a crucial part of a nation's past, no historian's education is complete. It is as absurd to suppose that the study of history can be based simply on an examination of the political past as to imagine that a view merely of the economic past is just as adequate. Moreover, the different methods which economic or social history require in investigating aggregate phenomena, together with the essential capacity for simple numeracy, cannot but widen and benefit the full educational value of studying history. British historians today are surely far less likely than formerly to react to such a diversity of approaches with the attitude typified by Hallam's earlier-quoted comment on Millar.[24] Much of both economic and social history must be of the 'philosophical' variety, if theories are to be tested against the evidence of a community's experience.

The notion that the subject is somehow a soft option must be totally destroyed; otherwise, it will become or remain one willy-nilly. Far better to be a hard option, attracting fewer students of high quality, than to remain the preserve of the mediocre, a haven for those inadequate at economics and unperceptive at history. Ill-equipped teachers, instead of responding in the manner of Waugh's fictional classics master, have been parading little more than a few generalized myths about the industrial revolution and supposing that this constitutes the economic history of Britain. Unless and until such procedures are banished from the subject, its intellectual reputation will suffer irreparably.

These desirable reforms will not in themselves necessarily ensure that economic history achieves or restores the appeal of readability. Dangers lurk on all sides. Too involved with economics and it can enter an arena full of disputations on method, conducted in a highly specialized language; too entangled with sociology and it can become cocooned in

[24] Above, p. 30.

polysyllabic jargon; too readily seduced by powerful historical personalities and it can abandon all heed of their social and economic context. Private languages favour private conversations and afford private contentment. But their resonance is limited. It is not accidental that the reformists have a more impressive literary performance than the neutralists. A moral message about heroes and villains, clothed in a vigorous or an elegant style, meets the demands of that overwhelming majority of history readers who are not professional historians far more readily than neutralist analysis, however lucid. If the subject-matter of economic history is indeed 'the typical representative or statistical fact, rather than ... the unique individual fact',[25] it is all the more difficult to convey its message to a wide audience. Who, the economic historian might ask, will buy my wares? Who wants statistics or economic models when they can enjoy indulgence in middle-class social guilt about profits, satisfyingly fed by a long tradition of Christian social teaching? Who wants analysis when the pleasures of narrative beguile?[26]

Such problems of content and presentation peculiarly beset the neutralist economic historian. For, dealing much in aggregates and analysis of economic phenomena, he may be more than usually prone to the fallacy of total objectivity in history. He may see himself as a 'neutralist', not simply in the sense used here, but as being capable of the moral neutralism of a supposedly 'positive' economics, of making objective, as distinct from normative, statements about history. A belief in this sort of 'scientific' history could readily ensure the alienation of a lay, as opposed to a professional, concern for the economic past. Economic historians, like other historians, search for truth and strive to maintain scholarly accuracy. But because they reach conclusions about, say, the consequences of

[25] T. S. Ashton, 'The Relation of Economic History to Economic Theory' in Harte (ed.), *Study*, p. 165.
[26] Reaction has already set in. See L. Stone, 'The Revival of Narrative', *Past and Present* 85 (1979), pp. 3–24; and for a counter-blast, E. J. Hobsbawm, 'The Revival of Narrative; Some Comments', *Past and Present* 86 (1980), pp. 3–8.

investment or the performance of an industry, sometimes by procedures very different from those used by other historians, they must not suppose that the result is necessarily a different sort of truth, immune either to reinterpretation or to moral judgement.

Moreover, economic historians, like other historians, need to remember that they exist and are allowed to pursue their pleasing vocation by the favour of a history-conscious society. History is said to be unpopular in Britain today. Certainly, in some influential quarters, the belief that it is bunk seems to have got a new lease of life; and certainly there are fears that many young people are growing up without any sense of the past. Nevertheless, it is likely that we are still a history-conscious society and that, for a majority of the people in this country, the past still has meaning. We look to it for evidence of the human spirit made manifest in a variety of ways; for a sense of identity and continuity; for the sources of achievement and failure; for the doings of individual men and women; for the joys or sufferings of groups, nations, or social classes; and for the unconscious working-out of the great themes of survival or decay. The economic past is but one element in that vision of the past which thus offers meaning to the present.

The great success of economic history, as a process of study and scholarship, is that it has mounted a victorious challenge to a once narrow vision of the past. It is an achievement for which generations of economic historians can be proud. Making and trading, the distribution of wealth, the economic results of population growth, the social effects of inflation: such matters and many more are now seen as rightful parts of that historical vision. The great challenge for economic historians today is to ensure that they retain their rightful and their comprehensible place therein. Otherwise, the economic past may well cease to have a future.

Index

Index